SELECTED POEMS

SELECTED POEMS

DAVID MUSGRAVE

EYEWEAR PUBLISHING

First published in 2021
by Eyewear, an imprint of Black Spring Press Group
Grantully, Maida Vale,
London w9, England, UK
United Kingdom

Cover design and typeset by Edwin Smet
Author photograph courtesy of Fairfax
Cover photograph by Getty images, Shark Bay, Western Australia

ISBN 978-1-913606-12-1

BLACKSPRINGPRESSGROUP.COM

God be gracious to Musgrave,
for he is a Merchant
— Christopher Smart,
Jubilate Agno, fragment C

David Musgrave was born in Sydney in 1965. After being awarded his doctorate in English literature for a dissertation on Menippean satire and the grotesque in 1998, he worked in IT before taking up a position teaching Creative Writing at the University of Newcastle in 2010. He founded the literary publishing house Puncher & Wattmann in 2005, at which he remains the managing director, and which has been the leading publisher of Australian poetry for the last decade. He has published seven collections of poetry and two audio CDs as well as a novel, *Glissando*. His work has been awarded, or shortlisted for, many literary awards in Australia. He lives in Newcastle, NSW with his family.

TABLE OF CONTENTS

1986–1999

BUDAPEST

There'll be Frank in Budapest, pathologically honest;
Wrapped in his old coat and haunting the square,
Humming the tunes that Liszt hummed way back then.
He's a bastard Hungarian – his German grandfather called
The place 'Ofen' – Frank, holding his arm behind his own back,
Saying *I don't know*, or scratching the ground.

And that black-earth Danube slugs through valleys
History-thick, rending the city – parvenu
Pest and Mongol-ravished Buda, under
Precarious bridges, skirting the Turkish barbicans,
Past the river parks, grey-granite and evergreen.
At least, I've never seen it –
Only swollen tanks crushing signposts,
Lurching, photographic. We had our own
Rebellion, in Olympic '56:
Water-polo played in a red Russian blood pool.

And St. Stephen's basilica (with his hand in St. Sigismund's),
The corduroy hats and flower embroidery blossoming,
And rust-black street railings marching, dull grey cobbles
With cracks cobwebbing – potatoes on sale for a pittance,
And motorized barges, the Magyar pride, and Frank, there.

I'll be there too, and Mano, cool, saying, *bloody*,
Giving a speech when he's drunk, performing for friends,
Blotto under a grotto the stars only hear about.
Greg and Bronwen will walk down the Andrassy Ut.
She polite and he indifferently rude,
Squaring his shoulders and rolling a string-leaf smoke.
Bronwen will sit on the riverbank, nursing her thoughts
Of the dual monarchy, plaiting her hair or falling

Asleep – she always falls asleep, and I
Will write, or hear some crazy story in
A language I can't understand.
                                        We'll meet Frank and Mano,
On street corners, intermittently; and in between,
Greg and I strut the streets or shuffle through leaves
In thoughtful oblivion.
                                Those beautiful streets!
Lunging like dinosaurs, through trees, up hills, dumb.
The symphonic skies with lilting cloud-rack, drifting debris
From Vienna, erstwhile hub of Empire.

We'll remember sad stories that made us say, 'God!',
Or made our eyes sting, just near the lachrymal duct, painfully,
We'll drink, on wistful afternoons, the wine
That tastes like a burnt out barrel, destroying notions
Of Bacchic peace and whirling nostalgia, orbiting
Over parks in the colours of mists.
We'll be lying on park benches, with spidery trees,
Their leaves on loan to summer,
Cold dankness wet underfoot.

We'll embrace in Budapest, in Hungary,
Behind the Iron Curtain, in some new position,
Hungarian kissing, forgetting the people who taught the
Importance of memory, persuasion and bulk-buying.
Mano and Frank will talk about medical matters,
Greg will listen, attentive, slyly uncorking another bottle,
And Bronwen, too, will be listening, almost pensive,

And I'm the obliging host in a foreign hotel room.

We'll go to the building that holds the museum,
And look up ethnography, and numismatics, and other terms
Incomprehensible, then see the Duna, the Danube,

From Fisherman's Bastion, peering at that ancient heart,
Backed by vineclad hills.

The city beneath our feet and enclosing us:
A carpet that runs up the walls and colours the sky
A lapis-lazuli owl-spotted dawn. We'll all
Take it in. I'll gaze on Bronwen in her riverside bliss
And Greg'll be howling a song about squash racquets,
Writing poems on dockets and wine labels, scratching his furious
Hair, or cantoing daily, will sing until the words fall apart.
Whatever it costs, there'll be someone to do up the adding,
A Mr. Hungarian or a chartered accountant, the sort
With the serious glass-frames, manic speck eyes, paper-drawn,
Ogling scribbles.

When it all comes waffling down, exhaling
After the final fling, when our visas run out,
And the sun spatters its final slow murmuring protest,
When cellos and tin-tacky harpsichords are tucked away in their crates,
The fish guzzle mud and the occasional hook,
We'll all catch a different streetcar –
When birds nailed to trees come all of a sudden alive in the flappity tempest,
And hair plumes in tickling droplet-cold wind,
We'll all meet at that next place our diaries say,
Scrawled hastily, lucid and bold.

1986

SONG

In the negative steam of a morning,
a Greek father chills his toes
and a pungent mug of coffee

on his verandah, watching a mother
and child pass, discussing dawn
business with his son.

The mother passes the message
of frost scrawled on the windows,
the greed of a truck at the lights,

to a house where her lover sleeps,
where a dog has pissed on the carpet,
where the etching of mice mark the walls.

Here in the house of the moon
with pink-shell earlobe walls,
in darkness she unwinds her scarf.

Here, where a kitten cries
and the smell of a biscuit factory
steals over a tight canal

she waits for doubt to decay,
for the mesh of day to unfold,
for the hunger of hunger.

In the chaos of innocence
her daughter pinches and plays,
giggling the signs of the ram,

tasting the name of dirt,
testing the sounds of an idiot,
teasing the patterns of ants.

Her mother, in time, is watching
under the flames of leaves
sunlit and still waiting.

1987

AFTER A STORM

A daughter is walking and dragging her father behind;
pillowing nimbuses rise in suffocating piles,
and look! Wonderful animals scavenge in madness!
They walk over dead leaves and grass
past white cars and a rippling bay.
The daughter and a dog engage in meaningless dialogue.
In some sunless lane
jacaranda blooms have fallen and been crushed,
oozing sour odour.
Airplanes whistle and roar and a jolting truck
starts like a hungry lover.

The father picks the daughter up,
tackles the gentle breast of a hill,
bathes her in an empty house,
puts her to bed in a room with a lino floor –
the whispering windows yield to the night
and the nervous conviction of more days
like snakes sliding past each other
in yawning heat.
The father fumbles into sleep
between cold sheets
before the wasting evening wastes away.

1988

ODE TO MICHAEL DRANSFIELD

Smack put you on the
rack stretching truth from
spasms gone amok.

Out of nothing came
nothing much, mere
words, coy evasions:

there were admiring parents
before their children died
too, o Chatterton.

Your life was a shopping list,
begun at the top, chucking
out the crap, ending with

poetry. You led
a stoned parade through
the supermarket aisles

of life, with hordes of little
Australian poetry boys
cheering, squealing *o captain,*

my captain while darkness
sneered like the hell
hound on heat you are.

1991

GLENROWAN

Strung up, punch-drunk and drooping, Joe Byrne fails
before the camera. And falls again. Exposed once more
are laughter and death – the puppetty fall,
the other charcoal grins on beds of bark.
The last coals die, the hotel still defies
extinction. Barbecue breath hangs in the morning.
The blackened torsos, the stumps would point
a way: windows, the sky, impossible flight.
Still they mill, the many are dead
tired and sick, for a time, the shooters
and those dead set on shrouds and decent burial.
Someone smokes, some twos and threes chew
the fat, and filmy smoke has made the trees betray –
that they're themselves, but better – growth,
defiance, decay. Down the way the tin man
falls as well. Anger breaks, retreats,
winters in another fresh fog. Among the hills
houses stoke their chimney pyres and the photographs
remain and for want of nothing better stories
dribble out over the years, forgetful of the mad
inventiveness of death, beyond the laughter of those
chargrilled statues, unfinished works, another joke.

1992

THE DEAD

for my father

He has come back.
He has come from outside himself to assume
the proportions of dream, in a city of symbols falling
from deliverance, offered up to speech.
He mouths voiceless vowels, but cannot settle
in the complex room with unwashed windows
and sparse light in starfish and jellyfish shapes,
moving between moments. He is the sovereign
of helpless beauty, full of advice and all
dressed up with nowhere to go. Tears are not
required, there is not long, there is no need
for reassurance. Pigeons scrape the eaves.
He moves about restlessly, smiling
as if he had given himself over
to the sea or the lobes of harbour underlapping
the sky. Books are of no consequence,
he can no longer read. He understands
the weather and is interested in me.
Nights come by, from time to time, but mostly
days with a hard yellowness fix themselves
in his eye. He wears the clothes of a family
man and has no need for food. He needs
only a little time, enough for love.
He only wants to talk.

1994

HISTORY

Where I have never been
I let myself go –
the Pacific: utopic, a stinging newness
in Magellan's eye;
a bunch of peasants armed with sticks
descends on local strongholds,
strangled with rage;
an eagle drops a tortoise on a poet's head
and Urquhart dies laughing.
We run into the same dead ends
too young to understand
(we are always too young, except in history)
until we reach that cul-de-sac and turn around to hear
a million, billion souls
crying *poormouth*, crying out in astonishment
Look! – it's the great unknown,
it's the other and its mother,
it's two friends conspiring among the jealous lakes
to make factory songs in a lyrical frenzy.
It's years and days and layers of pie
laid out for the moveable feast
to which we have been invited by
a bickering, gracious host demanding that we speak,
inviting with a loving smile the disagreements
on which we turn.
These are grand days,
when we discover the meaning of finality.
In the end, we are divorced from ourselves,
fearful of the sudden exile,
the grand sweeping exit,
the rehearsed line, the tragic gesture or
the silent spasm.

There is, after all, the chance to return
as ourselves, once again,
in that slippery fall.
And there is that other opportunity
to creep up over that ridge
and be blinded by the bright violence
of another shimmering sea.

1996

GENRE

(On sitting down to watch Kosky's *Lear)*

Shit happens in ways that continue to define
the imagination: a gesture bearing the weight of an age,
the acquiescent rebel who succumbs but will not die.
The simplest kind begins with words: a suitcase, neatly
packed with odds and ends, a conscience perhaps and a potpourri
of smells and mismatched buttons which, when unpacked, defy all order.
There are the bigger genres too: *The History of the West*
In Odorama – ask the scatological wunderkind –
Schwankspeare never smelt so good. And, it seems, there's magic,
although if it hasn't been expelled it's on the nose,
for sure. These days Horror has the upper hand. What else
can get a laugh when your heart-rate has gone completely spastic?

The commonplace, however ... the right place and the wrong time:
frangipani on the morning of a funeral,
envy bringing to light forgotten, unexpected jewels,
the ghost of sentiment returning in a dream, a passionate
logic, just when you thought it was safe to go back in the psyche.
Everyone sleeps as they should, each according to their demons.

1998

FROM *ON REFLECTION* (1992-1995)

Transient flesh and the buds of death
bloom on mercator window-panes, rippled
in convex heat, off on the dark road
of the shivering heart of ugliness
for the soft glimpse of cragged basins
of the south where porpoises gnash
water, blind fists whacking the shimmered
plate of sea unblinking, melting
into mirrors like that abstract desolation,
for months that ogle each other,
wondering but knowing how it will stop
in that creased night of chance
when the mice will leap and dance.

He walks across the road and sees his distorted reflection in a shop-front window. As with all grotesqueries, the tenor of his thoughts turns toward the pastoral and the eternally returning wake of cyclical death and heat. At this juncture comes the realisation that thoughts leading from each other and about each other have a morbidity that can only be resolved by an awkward humour that never fails to value the importance of stupidity as a guiding principle at all the critical cusps of life. Consequently, when he returns home, instead of writing he plays a mindless computer game.

Borne up and strewn with petals of decay,
their fleshy odour mourning the slow passage
through the dying day,
scattered by the failing breeze,
tottering from side to side,
carried by weak, sunburnt hands
to that narrow bower where the thin trees hum
and camellias lie bruised in falling light,
soft onto that mound where the cool grass spreads
and the ants already with their furtive gifts
begin their slow campaign, enveloped in
that cloudless afternoon, their frail embrace
about those hollow sockets in that grim face.

The death of yet another chance to snatch motivation from the jaws of sloth proves to be the inspiration for a reverie concerning the cinematic ritual and sensuality of a hero's death. Of course, he is his own hero, fighting virtual demons in the hope that he may get his dignity back, or at least an ideal free lunch. As is to be expected, closure proves elusive and death less than final: yet again the computer has defeated him. Inexorably, his thoughts turn to love.

Revert, abstract and feel fantastic for whole
days free from the taint of failure and free
from tongues chanting mantras,
seeing things in rocks, refusing white slippers.
If you do not, the grotto will close, denying
all images, shutting out those breezy
observances that come from air and the rhythm
of trees. The beyond is impossible to reach:
slinking shadows disappear with the day,
falling on lucid ponds and over leaves
infested with snails slowly mutilating
subtle shades, echoes of that voice
that comes from nowhere, rending all
that once seemed strange and magical.

Not being all that tired, he stays up late to watch a film about Saint Bernadette of Lourdes. She believes in the visions she has had in a grotto, just as he once emphatically believed in a world of the mind and used to be able to assert this belief with conviction. She refuses to wear white slippers to the grotto, as he refuses to call himself 'poet.' Perhaps the grotto is like that cave which is full of images but really a negative of how we are. It is beautiful, but such beauty is not like other forms of beauty that we deem 'good'. Rather, it is a revelation of banality, mortality and tiredness. Time for bed.

Podsnap to barstool, skunked in gimcrack hotels
with the remembrance of that wave of sickness,
Mexican style, inside the centrifuge where
fanciful outlines merge in violet richness.
Tip-toe to treetop, autumn flecks of lava
blazing in plumes of cocktail-coloured madness;
sepals unyielding, dense in foldless night of
camera-ready spurts of beauty flush with
fever-room outbursts stretched from thought to nightmare;
units of noise emerge like secret handshakes,
common enough but nothing more than islands,
pockets of forethought, outcrops, magma turned to
stone in the mouth of meaning, speechless tongues of
igneous petals grandly saying nothing.

He awakes not quite knowing where he is, although it is much like the half-dream room where the snakes squeal and the alligators blow trumpets. Of course, he is in his own bed and of course he is alone and slightly hungover, and he purposely slides into the semi-directed dreams, a grotesque of nightclubs and forests, volcanic lust and, if it is the case that some people can speak in tongues, hearing in ears. Eventually, sleep yields no more slack, and he must get up. He potters around, avoiding making his bed out of procrustination: that is, putting off making one's bed in case one has to lie in it. The fuzziness of his morning merges into a general fuzziness, around which he cannot seem to find his way.

Prone to tears and boredom because summer
was not extraordinary, peeled back
like an afternoon hat, survivor of heat
and unseasonal winds, like friendliness,
fresh and unforgotten. Out of sorts
later that night, darkness piles on cool
tea leaves pungent in secret diagonal
gardens sprayed with kamikaze beetles.
From the hidden corners odours grow:
bubblegum port-wine magnolia, privet
like rancid fat, the layered tannin, hopeless
dandelion aglow with twilight breeze.
Even on those days of total eclipse
dark fruit bursts like passion between your lips.

Despite grief, its process taking the course of any disease, that tarot joy of living still remains, even if the pleasure it offers is no longer familiar. There are some moments when he is hopelessly happy, balanced also by those moments on the edge of the pit. He is spending most of his time in unhappy holiday mode, mooning around his mother's house. He disappears from time to time into books, and sniffs the odours of the house that have long since ceased to be real, like the tumuli of tea leaves that cover the camellia bed.

For every action there is an equal and opposite
revulsion,
embryos in ultrasound,
serrated leaves that populate the picnic;
and for every slice of life
consumed –
medallions on a china plate,
time-lapsed growth and putrefaction
bound together in the ribboning mind –
another cut
in the adjectival theatre
going down the wrong way
and at another time altogether
made a meal of.

One night he watches a video of a contemporary movie that has putrefaction as one of its major themes. Even though the dialogue is terrible, he likes watching the maggoty images that pop up every few minutes. These, in turn are interspersed with documentaries about Life On Earth, and amputations. It makes fascinating viewing as he eats his dinner. After a few weeks of the cycle of videos, remembrance, comfort and pain, he decides it is time to return to his own home and resume the practice of everyday life.

Dissent is like a poisoned alphabet
that spells the names of multiplied obsessions
speckling the refrigerator door.
Their messages reflect the accidents
of time and space: the algebra of distance
and the arguments of broken memory
quarrel on the page like yowling cats.
This disagreement turns on decadence,
as with poetry, dedicated
to those lazy cracks that act out
passions, tranquilized politenesses
and callous insincerities calmly
placed upon the page, miraculously
taking on the semblance of a life.

The next day he gets a postcard from his brother who has just arrived in Korea for an intensive language course. Ah Seoul! *he reads and sticks it on the fridge next to the other cards from Paris, Tokyo, New York and Newcastle NSW. He enjoys reading them almost as much as he enjoys writing and sending them, his preferred medium being the back of a beer coaster. Along with the postcard comes a telephone bill and a letter offering him a job at a nearby university. It's only casual tutoring, but he can't complain. In fact, thanks to the incompetence of the university administration, the letter gives him only a week's notice. He decides to see the place the following day, ironing a shirt and having an early night so that the visit to his new place of employment cannot possibly go wrong.*

Everything must have a name: the ant's pants,
the termite's trousers, that acme of acne, the moon.
There are right-handed feelings and left-handed feelings
and ambidextrous thoughts of great cunning.
There are objects in the dative case
and actions that assume a feminine form.
There are names of names of names of names
and fish and empty windows and those full.
There are days obsessed with the memory of smell
and curves of various velocity.
There is the irritating need for food
and a modicum of space and peace and quiet.
Obviously, life is so wonderful
it's a wonder everyone has not been driven mad.

He resolves never again to use the first person pronoun in any future poems, a determination arrived at after socialising with his friends, drinking, playing games, talking about incunabula and becoming rather appalled at the inescapable necessity to assert one's self, even if it only takes the form of defending one's head against an angry pool cue in the local pub. Generally, he observes that he has not laughed so much in months and is overwhelmed by the feeling (deluded) that he has escaped. He drives back home via the same circuitous route and drops in on his mother on the way.

If it isn't one thing it's another,
laughter without end, enough to make a cat speak.
And, if the door does not stay shut, it opens
on an inside that has shrunk and an
outside that cannot be admitted:
gnocchi clouds float in a blue soup,
white noise in the television sky;
a high wind flays the trees
and papers inside scatter and reel.
It is like a double dream, that which is written
and that which we dream of as we write.
In the end, in the dark, it may be the case
that a lonely figure is out there, somewhere,
throwing stones from the outskirts of night.

The bushfires have spared them this time and once the ashes have been raked from the garden life appears almost normal. Everything reminds him of everything else, so he makes an effort to try and pin a bit of certainty onto the world. Neither astrology nor alienation, speculation nor chiromancy can provide the spur he needs to seize his life by the scruff of the neck and toss it out on the street where it probably belongs. He returns to his squalid little flat for the start of a new week.

Such are the wonders of nature: almost transcendent
blue sky and a pair of crooning reptiles,
distant cousins of stone emitting alien
lullabies on a rocky altar hard
by the edge of a blind land – o desire,
flowing out of itself yet perfectly formed
each and every time, mistaken for
the song of love or fear of the sea or pity
for a becalmed ship mooning the horizon.
On other days hordes of gulls wheedle
and shriek and cold waves strike the shore.
This is the limit, where foam flies and rocks
endure the sea and various creatures slide
in and out as smoothly as machines.

The next day is decidedly ordinary. He wants to enrich his measly existence with culture-vulturing at the art gallery (he has called his pseudo-girlfriend but she is most emphatically not in.) There are some surreal works on show, Magritte's being his favourite. Before one particular painting he is transfixed – the combination of beauty, the inexplicable and the incongruously familiar almost moves him to tears. He has arranged to meet his Irish friend later at their local. From the bus the city looks as though it is populated by mad Futurists. It probably is.

The rules decree *thou shalt be happy*
days full of tragic complexity
overwhelmed by laughter.
Too many paths that could be gone down
resolve into one path marked only by years
piled like stones by the side of the road.
Beyond ordinary meanings
other sentences unfurl themselves
like eternal flowers
dandled by the heavy breeze
breathing life into the speechless past
flatly denied by the teeming present
and passing, with forgiveness, to the future.

Aside from the fact that from time to time life seems to be a very long snuff movie, he emerges from a daydream to look at the page before him. This is what it's all about, he decides, the white page, the endless choice. On the way home he found a lobster (twenty dollar note) on the ground – O lucky day! – with which he was able to buy himself a lotto entry, a lottery ticket, some marinated olives and artichoke hearts for a salad. When will my luck run out? *he asks himself as he eats his lunch over the sports section of the newspaper.*

2000–2011

FROM *TO THALIA* (2004)

LAGOON

This is where I come from if it's true
to say I come from somewhere not just
anywhere south of the imagination
like warty hills of the Monaro
or an Irish quag.
It's Lagoon with wind-tussocked, wrinkled
hills worn down to a murmur
that claims me.
Flat-skied, convict-shaped
earth, the barren sweep
from Tannas Mount knuckled
with Bathurst quartz, small and obedient
noon shadows: this is where justice
jammed them, impatient and impenitent
forebears transported for a brace
of crimes: possession
of a stolen lamb,
highway robbery
and other, nameless filchings cancelled
by oblivion.
It's hard to tell exactly where
it was: the lagoon has forgotten
itself, drowned
under Chifley Dam's
green skin brailled by metallic rain,
or a mired bend in Campbell's River
where dragonflies whirr in a spectral frenzy
like solid drops of petrol darting in the sun.
I have inherited their future

born of silent massacres,
patient weathering
of the cold fastness of hills
and endurance of each summer's baked mirages.
They mastered the art of sticking
to the narrow furrows of their lives
whereas I have learnt
only the art of streets,
sailing between their guttered shores
on that new ocean, traffic.
Every trace of them has vanished.
There is a school there now,
where children, yet to learn
that dreams are what make death real,
play in the stark sun.
Horse studs
gather along the creek
and they stand there, fluid
flanks shiny in wintered light
chewing and staring down
impostors in their midst.
Time has stolen it,
evaporated family mysteries
like the slow death of a photograph
of the old farm,
like neap days
pinched of history.

MINNEAPOLIS

America, you've laid a cable in my heart
with fifty million channels showing beer and cars
and porn. I watch them all with bored fascination,
a world within a world and yes, I am a part-

time businessman learning how to think
in an American accent, out to lardy dinner
before the big game mascot masquerade, a super-
market carnival that's sponsored by a drink

as difficult as opera to enjoy but fizzier.
In the mini-Apple sky the clouds are bruised purple
by searchlights, Go Vikings! and there's evidence of thought
bubbles bursting as they rise above the sober

clink of glasses filled with water and leaking words
that pass for conversation, here in Hiawatha's
Hideaway on Nicollet and Thirteenth Streets
with Cindy, Larry, Rich and Sandy, our team of experts

on digital manipulation, imaging and scanning
(documents, primarily). It's the end of a long
project, Sandy on fulfillment, Larry, hardware,
Cindy, programming and Rich, project planning,

while I just write the cheques and wander through the warehouse
district every lunchtime down to the chocolate milkshake
of the Mississippi churning towards St. Paul
and watch as the glacier belt winds arrive and douse

the flaming leaves of yet another Indian summer.
To the skyways! A floating island docked at mezzanine

level, a city within a city riddling the heart
of the grid with portholed shopping tubes from which a number

of minor wonders can be seen: stainless steel
art museums, Minnehaha Falls, a giant
spider's egg about to burst from Hubert Humphrey
Metrodome. I'm keeping my end of the deal;

My nape please, says Cindy as we're walking home,
meaning: massage it. These people cannot mourn;
our bedroom is a furnace. *My nipple is my Naples*,
she cries and rides me steady as a metronome.

DEW

for Ben Fenton-Smith

None are more familiar with dew
    than professional footballers. From early
grades they are used to running through
    practice drills and hurling their burly
frames through rucks while the moist chaff
    of wet grass under winter lights
softens their fall, accustoms the half-
    back to the slippery ball and writes
green cuneiform on wet sandshoes.
    And they fear it. All of them dread
kicking off the dew in the twos
    because they forgot what the coach said.
Half their lives are spent in clouds
    of condensation or the cold heat
of a winter sun where even the crowds
    seem like droplets on the concrete
rose of the stadium. In the final days
    of their season, sweat-spangled on the eve
of their triumph, the ball on a string and their plays
    honed, even the doubters believe.
And the last day is, once again,
    already an aftermath: the ground's been shaved
and sucked dry by the noon sun
    and the paddock has become a paved
and bristled hell for those who will
    collide with it and pinion flesh on
earth, earth on flesh and spill
    blood for the sake of a game. Possession
is the law; all are possessed.
    And when the crowd melts into the dry
darkness, after that great red football's

booted between the uprights of the sky-
scrapers and gone, the sky bawls
cheerless little drops for the victors
and decks the oval with the losers' jewels.

MALUA BAY

Buried nose-first in sand and filling the headland
like the layers of a cake squashed sideways, these rocks

appear to have dive-bombed the beach and crashed
the sea's party, burying their heads for shame leaving

their tails exposed to scale and scatter, much as that other
party, all but dead save igneous embers and sleeping

bags bunched with drunks, trails beer cans in its wake.
The world is sometimes like this, parodying life;

at other times it's sending itself up: the rocks are waves
solidified mid-slide, their foam a quartzed ridge

eaten out by the sea, a shock of crabs satirising
the sunken splendours of the bay. But when uninvited

party guests plagiarise the rocks, the sea, whatever,
it all gets complicated, as when television

mocks the stars and the stars wink back as if to say
that they wouldn't have it any other way.

JELLYFISH

for Catherine Parer

… woke up to a green sky full of jellyfish
streaming in on a south-easterly swell,
tentacles flapping
election posters on heritage chimneys
in Sydney Park like summer curtains
invaded by a southerly change.
Far below, the sound of popping
bacon and a crackling bushfire
of eggs divided the morning into two
horizons: the frantic and the surreal.
Punters dashed from breakfast to vote
on the horses, voters to bet
on the politicians, while cruising
over pollarded trees hedged under the shallow,
inverted bell-curves of overhead wires,
the jellyfish drifted north-north-west, their shadows sinking
whole suburbs in rippling eclipse. A pod of humpback
paddy wagons wailed in ragged pursuit.
Out on the tiles
of the sky's swimming pool
others followed on foot, eyes fixed
on the trembling medusae, decapitated
heads trailing ectoplasm
out to Windsor, towards the dead
centre, nerveless, dangling disasters throwing
spanner after spanner into the works
of polling day. Risking the fluffy
mines of cloud-fields, riddling
watery topaz with gelatinous confetti,
the jellyfish sent shudders
through a nation caught between

the choice of more of the same with less fun
or less of the same with more boredom
narrowly, by preferences, in the marginals.
In the capital, old jellyback himself quivered
over the question of their legal status,
scrambling the air force, invoking
the spectre of revolution by unreason
while on and on the jellyfish nudged
and surged serenely into the wind, imperial
at their purple core.
All this I saw
on election day, promenading my lobster,
with blue hair and mixolydian eyes...

THE MUSEUM OF OPEN AIR, OBERON

Bone's lichen and wood's ossified splinters
gibber under slack fences, sunk in a carapace
of leaves. Trees strike down into the earth:

sky amputates their limbs. The grey confluence
of bone on wood remains an undertow
in the busy grassy sea. Premonitory

trees circle the hills, shading hidden
kangaroos and sunk in anger at lantana's
inelegant green. Clouds sweep aside the sky,

November wind and a waterfall's spray
collide in the spun fragrance of spring; rivers of
dry wood run across the wounded face

of hillsides reefed with anthills. Shoals
of seeds awash in the world's museum testify
against complacency: even here you may

find yourself scuttling among the statues,
withered skeletons of trees and livid rocks,
and under them the waterfall plundering silence.

TO THALIA

for Peter Kirkpatrick

1.

These days poetry's all about extravagance:
like the way a string of sausages
impersonates an approaching train and promises
a full belly for some, lateness for another
and for others yet again that they've missed
the same old, same old and discovered instead
the tail of everybody else's head –
like how dawn in the west means darkness
in the east; or it's like a guitar
of harbour ripples, two overlapping
pennies mourning the passing of another
super tanker; or like how a fart
makes castanets of buttocks, or a pool table
reincarnates Heraclitus, even if
we are not gods, or at least, not yet

2.

despite the enormous coat-hanger pegging
out a highway between two pylons and hanging
empty air, or the scattered dice of selfish
waterfront apartments, remnants of a god-
sized game of 'Room-with-a-view-to-die-for' that's been
played to death. And no one is laughing – rats
among the chandeliers flash gold teeth
and their leathery wives wrinkle slitty eyes.
Only their champagne bubbles burst with laughter,
but don't let that fool you. There are other,
less fun games: trains are incompetent
games of billiards, cannoning but never scoring

and out of the corner of my eye the city
plays hide-and-seek with the back of my head.
But these are distractions only, like all games

3.
where winning can be dismissed as an act of grace
and losing an unnecessary annoyance.
It's a bit like knowing it's all bullshit
but doing it anyway. Or is it like you, Thalia,
reaching out a crook from stage left
to pull off those acts past their use-by date
and peeking cheekily from the wings, mouthing,
Did you like that? Should I do it again?
If only you would do it more! And give
something to the over-confident skyscrapers
to think about, if the novice acupuncturists
of the city skyline can be said
to think at all. The sky receives the therapy
it needs and arches its back gratefully above us,
mood heavenly. And we're thankful: indolent

4.
days are better than *dies irae* – except when
you abandon us, Thalia, pack up your mask
and leave us with only the laughter of politicians
(an oxymoron, I know) and the sideways anti-
clockwise D, or upside-down smile
of the bridge. A slowly swaying yacht
recovers its silvered mast from the water
and casts it out again. The harbour is full
of blue beer and the sun is an extra
whose wages have been paid by the yachties.
It's the end of a long shoot. Seagulls

interrupt the afternoon's rehearsal
of autumn with shrill asides; they're a gesture
stolen from a cocktail party, let loose
in the sky to their own wheeling applause.
Ferries circulate through the bloodstream

5.
of the port, commuter-positive
and a computer crashes into the sea
of information and sinks without trace.
But there is always a trace, isn't there,
Thalia, to remind us of the other
selves we've become and, even without
you, there is still your Cheshire Cat
smile. In the distance a child's mosquito
whine starts up and those tiny muezzins
siphon off my happiness, erecting
fragile minarets up and down
my bare legs and arms. Somewhere a baby
is crying with a mouth like a torn scone
and it still seems vaguely funny, like a miracle
cut out of the back of a Cornflakes packet:
because these days we're accustomed to seeing
God only in the heads of our beers

6.
(Bernhard) and rainbows cause tooth decay
(Garcilaso de la Vega). I've had it
with this city. It's all sneer and veneer,
isn't it Thalia? That's why I have to write
to you, because you're elsewhere. And there's not
much choice: Canberra is a hospital
with the roof taken off; Adelaide's the dark side

of the moon, a regimented folly (Bail),
and Brisbane, well, it's not much better than steam
on stilts – too hot but not as far away
as Perth and less unspeakable than Melbourne.
But that's no reason to fail to choose another
city. Each one has its shitty gems,
a camel sniffing at the rail with a resentful
nostril (Brodsky) or the rotting fingers
of Walsh Bay's piers gloved by the harbour.

7.
That's the reason why you were last of the Muses,
Thalia – comedy must saunter in
behind the rest and mercilessly take
the piss out of history and hymns,
of tragedy, erotica, the lyric
and astrology, of music, dancing
and that clunker, epic – please don't baulk
at being told by me what you should do:
just do the opposite (bravado's the key).
That's the reason why you should be here:
last continent, first city, chock-
a-block with gritty charms like sluggos
clogged with sand after a savage dumping;
and, in the distance, there's a gum-ringed field
I could buy after decades of nine to five
and then fester in, more bald than alive.

8.
So here I am on an Erskineville verandah
under the airborne moss of a jacaranda
floating above my head at night – and still
I keep returning to the harbour, jagged

wet caiman snouting the humid plain
of Sydney because I can't be anywhere else,
Thalia, I'm snookered in this dumb city
of brilliant hazards and dull comparisons
with Rio, San Diego, et cetera dice
me with boredom. But one of these days
you'll come waltzing in through the heads
of my imagination (Krishnamurti)
and that will suffice to slay them in the aisles
and flay the cured hide of this city,
unearthing at last its pink nascent laughter.

BLACKHEATH

My memory is of imagining
a Nissen hut on a scrubby hillside
as we hairpinned our way up
to Blackheath, perhaps for me
for the first time. I must have been three.
The house was nothing like it.
It was waiting for us, brick
and wood and an iron roof
that echoed with the sky
drilling into it each time it rained.
What I loved most was the indeterminate
room between the bathroom and the kitchen
and its brown linoleum, a grotesque pattern
as regular as city blocks
with ferns and sylvan diamonds
involuted in its borders.
I drove cars through it.
From the back doorstep river rocks
flowed in cemented tessellations, a complex
proposition for the Batmobile. The path spread out
through the cool garden and its sparse lawn,
islands of rhododendron and azalea,
and around the corner where footsteps rippled
and rang between the sunroom and the garage.
A peaceful sea lingered in the high trees
and pine cones fizzed and popped
on the spokes of branches
and landed in the damp shadows.
Each morning my grandfather's axe sounded
and resounded from the shed
while the smell of freshly baked bread
is all that remains of my grandmother.

As the sun climbed higher than whisked cirrus
the gulping echo of currawongs
gonged and the silver sun
bounced off the roof like the clash of blinding cymbals.

Blackteeth, we called it later.
Tea leaves accumulated under an azalea
just like at home.
A Dennis Lillee of the night,
I measured the run up to my bed
through the living room as far as the dark
sunroom and then, racing past the television
I leapt into the sunken, musty sheets.
Later, when I woke in the dark
in a warm pool of piss,
before I'd call out to my mother
I could hear the living room clock,
its patient tick and chirr
as it amassed its hours
and sank into the future.

POSTCARDS FROM A DROUGHT

1\.
A pair of exercise bikes
parked on a concrete slab
in the front yard of the house
in the middle of the harrowed plain.

2\.
Bore water lashing
the grass and the daisies,
a green iris
in a bloodshot eye.

3\.
Umbrella grass lost
in the corners of sheds,
piled high to the ceilings:
an ossuary of fine, spoked bones.

4\.
A busy highway
beginning somewhere out back
ends at the biscuit jar,
jammed with ants.

5\.
A bust of Voltaire
smiles too much
in a dusty sunroom
stacked with leather suitcases.

6.
Wood pigeons and wasps
drink from the covered bathtub.
Lowing warily, starved of grass,
cattle graze the lawn.

7.
Bowsers of oats, water,
petrol. From the road,
fine dust storms leap
over them and vanish.

8.
Eight linked maidens
dance around the outside
of a stained cement urn. Frogs
inside it croak like prophets.

9.
Making love in the afternoon,
trying for a child; almost at random
white butterflies flower
over coarse lawn.

10.
Venus wakes us up at 3am
intruding among the trees
and then ascending,
dwindling.

11.
On the fourth day of Christmas
crows rise
from pepper trees
staining the grid, the dust.

12.
A dead tree quivering:
a bird springs into
a bush. And then resumes
its funerary.

13.
Cyclone wire. A blue-tongued
lizard garrotted attempting
a rhomboid. A storm
of ants at its head. Clear sky.

14.
Wires have disappeared
from the telegraph poles.
Everything goes underground
in this heat.

15.
Sundial in shadow,
spare clouds drift.
Buried at its base,
grandparents' ashes.

16.
An ancient woman forgets
the name of her daughter-in-law.
Wet ice slips
in an empty wine glass.

17.
In the distance cars hover
on liquid haze
and sink
into the dry road.

INTIMATIONS AT WERRIS CREEK

Dense syllables, trees
and the breath of a grey fire:
the train hurls us
at evening. Yellow
trucks hurtle the other way.
The carriage is filled
with teenagers, flushed
with reluctant arrival
and kangaroos. They sing
ABBA as the hills bud
dark cattle and tarnished
silver dams slice
into soft slopes.
Bones of dead trees
rhyme with a fence;
above yellow walls,
an iron red roof
pitches into darkness
and the earth rises up
under the trees,
under the pale evening.
They let their reflections
stain the carriage windows,
their words allowing the train
to speed up into darkness:
Mamma mia, here I go again…

GOOBRAGANDRA RIVER

Every time I come here it's the same
elastic band of the imagination
humming between the city
and the bush with a sound like swarming
traffic and tensed like the futures
exchange before a war. Rocks, bloomed
with lichen, stud the hillsides and an ancient
violence has shredded some trees, flung limbs
cantilevered above the path. A stream fleeced
with ripples spoils over rocks: you can drink
from the gathering shudder of bubbles
clear offerings of the mountain, above the mild tattoo
of twigs snapping underboot hear
a small waterfall exhale noisily.
At the end of the stamped track the river surges
over its bed of smooth and roughly milled
pebbles like the hide of a fabulous reptile
or its eggs. Skimming across the river's surface
medallion-sized stones until bored,
just like in the city, you shanghai
rocks the size of fists and lacerate
its skin, holes punched through to see
who can make the biggest splash.

SKIMMING STONE

Shooting stars have a certain interest. They'd be even finer if it weren't for their tail. – Sei Shonagon

Intimate as a palmprint
the skimming stone weighs
a solid splash in your hand.

Each throw is like
a puckered thread
of kisses pulled from the water

or slaps teasing the patience
of the sea. But the sea
doesn't stir. In a cool

embrace it sucks each stone
down into itself as if
the stones were tongues,

down into the generous
depths where secrets lie:
leaping fish and the tunnelling

grace of dolphins rolling
out of the deep and stabbing
the surface with quick fins.

LAPS, COOK & PHILLIP POOL

Each turn you think, *it's just another lap*,
add one to the running total, or swimming
perhaps, wearing down to a tired slap

from the early laps when you were skimming
like a stone across the surface with each stroke.
This is when it's like a soup brimming

with broiled, meaty swimmers going for broke
leaving you interfering in their wake,
a self-stirring broth. But when you poke

beneath the surface it turns out it's a lake
with band-aid reeds unanchored from the floor
and hairs coiled lazily as eels, and flakes

of skin suspended in the murk, the spoor
of these pudgy freestyle lobsters as they
tumble-turn, kick off the wall and bore

through the pewter water like a tray
of fleshy bottle-openers tipped into
a bathtub, arms flapping and cogged grey

necks tortoising angrily. It's too
efficient, too sufficient, these machines
of pumped sexuality pumping through

this pool, the harbour's playpen; it seems
like nineteen forty-two, the port swarming
with a squad of midget submarines,

only now they're leaving the water, warming
themselves in a shower then, ray-banned,
armoured in their pressed suits and disarming

with their ultraviolet smiles, these tanned
subs break the surface on each street
corner, fleshly invaders, oh so discreet.

FOR ZOE MARGARET FENTON-SMITH, ON HER CHRISTENING

A peach:

that's how you came into the world,
Zoe, your tiny head bruised and furzed
with ginger down, the fruit of your parents' love.
You've taught us how that flawed menace, the world
can offer up perfection, how by fleshing
out a thought you make it seem

to each

of us that you have always been
just how you are, and will be: minute, ancient
moons of your fingernails, the quiver
of your sleeping eyelids, your ear a fine shell
filled with the roar of living. A new star
blinked into being when you were born

among

the ageing constellations of your family
and friends. And even though you have the same
one-way ticket all of us are given,
it seems we're off in opposite directions,
like galaxies whirling apart from each other
at break-neck, red-shift speed. You're

blooming

towards that peak of beauty, youth:
from there you'll watch us shrivel to our ends.
But really, it's not so bad. Each day the world

gets smaller with each singlet you outgrow,
with each foray into the unknown and every
word you learn. And words are what keep

death

at bay. You'll explore mountains
and valleys of your fingerprints, discover
the fit of finger joint and nostril – and other fits
delightful and repugnant, like rhymes: college
and porridge, father and rather, silly and willy –
one day you'll learn the way in which

your breath

blooms like a fogged rose in winter is like
the way your life fills each of us with hope
and lets us peer through the mirror of our deaths
in your blue eyes into the wonderland
of planet Zoe. Today you have an audience,
the most indulging that you'll ever have

played

to, one who'll watch with loving wonder
your every gurgle, sniff, yowl and slobbering,
your rampant curiosity and your coy
craving for attention. You won't remember,
but we're here today to welcome you, Zoe:
welcome to the world in which you

were made.

FROM *WATERMARK* (2006)

WATERMARK

Never judge a book by its reader
unless it's the kind that's read by touch,
fingers skimming down the columns
as if shutting dead eyes. The language
in that book requires no translation
other than what it becomes, which is itself
plus desire. The days are flowing messily
as money, but without the usual muddle:
every drop accounted for, like how a puddle,
stamped on, sneaks back to form before
another step. If the earth is alive
the oceans are its eye. In another's hands,
the book is something else. Hold up to the light
the note, the stamp and it will bear witness.

PUDDLES

Before we met I used to walk for miles
each time it rained,
plashing myself through the teeming city
and its angry offscourings,
the wet footprints of the sky.

In those long, cold mirrors, diamond-shallow,
I saw my flattened stride
in the future of another puddle,
mussel soup, with which I courted

you one night, having forgotten how one puddle
leads always to another,
inchmeal deep

like windows stretched across the ground
and, behind them, in their stillness,
the sudden pooling of our lives.

THE FISHERMEN

Forgetting for a while or forgotten
by the company of women, the fishermen
come each Sunday to their dawn spots,
threading, rigging, casting out. What is it
draws them here? Is it protest or desire
pulling at the other end of the line?
Or is it when the line begins to sing,
snagged, snapping or fibrillating wildly?
No lamenting lost chances blunts
their appetite. Every catch is memorable
and every cast is palpable: the hiss
of a squid just landed, the rippling mobius
of an octopus or the mullet's dying thrash
and frothing. Every bait swiped only
eggs them on, the silent swish of schools
below the surface or the play of tailor
just beyond the beach. Then, like midwives
they begin again their preparations,
washing, tying, waiting for that struggle
to the surface of another difficult birth.

AUSTRALIAN BEACH PATTERN

Was this the dream in the year of Dunkirk? Captured on a beach,
the victory of perfection over beauty, the sun precisely
chiselling a tableau so extreme it chills. Look:
never-ending tubes of flesh glisten like an assembly
line of cocktail sausages and waves appear to open on the beach
like pages of a book
that's never read but flipped through on the coffee table sand.
A ghastly cherub flanks its towelling father, chubby hand
outstretched as if about to unleash song or introduce
art deco's ugly underbelly browning on the sand.
The father sports a wet cowlick that's eerily familiar
and above another father's head, a martial spade
raised sky-high by the infant on his shoulders
salutes the triumph of the will
to uniformity. Rubber-helmeted maidens aspire
towards a beach ball or admire
the fatherly parade
bravely marching into the sea.
In the shallows youths are studying the proper use
of pleasure, righting model
yachts or blowing up things. In the torso zoo
perfection has a name and number, fully realised by a pair
of sand-pailed breasts at lower left. On the rock above, a mother
balances a child between her knees,
handling it as if it were a specimen.
On this beach everything is true.
Out in the surf a man and woman are pretending to play.
He has one arm raised, as if to strike;
his other is forcing her down, bending her at the waist
back into the water. It's funny how evil always begins with bad taste.

FREEMAN'S REACH, HAWKESBURY RIVER

For J. W.

Out of the silence, a team of ducks
lands on the river with a whoosh
of compression braking, drowning
out the sound of cattle chewing
on the other bank. From around
the bend a speedboat lamely chugs
upstream, then turns away, its wake
a tightening knot on the river's stillness.

Unlike the river that matched
a perfect hill, the cross-hatched
mirror now glitters fuzzily.
Poplars quiver like yellow whips.
Bee-racked, rising out of thick grass,
castor-oil plants brandish their pods,
tiny red grenades armed
with green pins. Behind us,
a hill mined by rabbits bares
its guts behind a retaining wall
of chicken wire.
Half a rampart,
the ironbark jetty warps over water
and standing at its end, a poet
completely surrounded.

A GLASS OF WATER

Un seul verre d'eau éclaire le monde
– Cocteau

Behind the wedding couple, a mirror harbours
their reception.
Outside, from the verandah, the harbour mirrors
the exception
of city from sky, hills snug with houses

and a glass of water standing on the railing,
half empty or half full. In the failing

afternoon light
brightening buildings counterpoint the darkness,
glinting upside-
down inside the glass, and the newly-weds,
seen from outside

joining hand to hand for the wedding reel,
glide under its meniscus, head over heels.

WHALES, HEAD OF BIGHT

Upturned valleys or hulls
the colour of gun-metal
disappear in white flowers,

green tents bedded with petals,
basking snore-ends lolling
through spume banks for hours

on end, spy-hopping, rolling,
saluting the circling gulls
with flipper-toast wave breaches

and, sinking once more in mist-sighs
resume a cruising shoal
never at ease, a capsized

squadron still on patrol
while on their backs wet sunlight
burns in a dark-timbered blaze.

FROM *PHANTOM LIMB* (2010)

OPEN WATER

At last we got clear of the narrows
and headed out into open water,
shredding the rapid ocean into spray
until time became something that tasted
of salt, open like a sentence:
beat up, beat down, iambic swell.

Then the horizon downed the final wafer
of land and we entered the massive rocking
stillness of the deep and its sparking
serrations, shut down the engines and drifted.
The sun beat on everything, bleaching
the top of the sky and its anvils

of cloud and lit up the leap of flying fish
like daytime meteors darning the sea.
We were still and unalone. Trawlers
far to north chugged stern-heavy
back to port and beyond them tankers,
languorous sunbathers stretched out and waiting.

Out of this same illimited plain
the British had come, wind-stung and flawed,
laden with cargoes of concepts
and shadows, things which couldn't be seen
but assembled themselves, a ruling machine
intricated into the vast and difficult continent-factory

and worked out in angles of apple-bright
metals, a lunar rust and starbursts
of roads and houses and human geometries,
varicose gullies and othering fences,
the bullet's graph. These were the blood-lessons:
that something which does not yet exist

is not the same as nothing: folded deep
within ourselves are nuggets of future
and the shock of their dredging.
Sunlines speared the water as we tilted
and sprawled and trailed a line
and let currents age us, gently.

There were only two ways to go:
across to where we had been, would go,
or down, each almost forever.
But even the longest line will turn,
like our slow drift
leaving its scrawl on open water.

PHANTOM LIMB

My enemy reminds me of my father:
the smell of smoke and newsprint, and the eye

behind the lens. I cannot understand the likeness:
my father was kind,

but he, my enemy,
deceives me from his empty office;

besides, my father has been dead for fourteen years.
I haven't seen my enemy for one,

but a semblance persists. He is a length of mind
which has no end. He harvests anger

and his name is myth.
His limbs hang loose and powerless,

his reasons, features, falter into word-mist,
but still he hurts me with his snarling smile.

I dreamt of him the other night
– wood is ash's dream of being whole –

and when I woke, the only clue
to what I'd lost, like a tingling nose before the lie

was an itch where nothing itched before,
a phantom absence: the limb I never knew I had, excised.

GRASS

As I waded through paddocks of wallaby grass, nineawn,
windmill, umbrella, and curly Mitchell, I remembered
how I had felt like ripping my own face off.

I'd just flown through a free-fall
of stomach-unseating violence
from the city to a western plain and survived

for my annual face-off with *bucolia melancholia*.
I wandered there in a kind of grateful silence.
A powdery mind-black ribbon of falling

dark water was looping around from the south
nudging trees like a dog's black nose
with wet, cold wind

and then as it closed in, the sky's white mouth
opened, hushed then bawled once-in-a-decade rain.
Channels flexed their muddy sinews

and out in the dust-red yard
the earth spat up echoes of rain
and the slow leaks sped in the homestead roof's groined hollows.

When the rain cleared
the dense cloud had passed into a fine dust haze
disking the sun. New cloud roped

and five-minutes-to-seed grass
began to shoot
as the house was lowered slowly into darkness.

The oil-black smoke from the ululating flames
of the citronella lamps curled and awned
as I flickered inside the house

where the talk was of grass
and of making a killing
and where we would feast.

SOIL

The earth is growing in me, clump by clump,
a butting fastness, anchoring but intimate
as a scar, an out of bounds moving in.
Perhaps that's why dreams take longer,

lately, to wander out of, as morning tilts at noon
and hope resumes its blind battering.
Soon orbs of wet clay, once eyes
will scan and frame in this cave of bone,

but until then I'll keep on losing balance
as if half of me were air, the other ink
for a small obituary, or a small grimoire,
a B-grade movie prop scripted to burst into flame.

ON THE INEVITABLE DECLINE INTO MEDIOCRITY OF THE POPULAR MUSICIAN WHO ATTAINS A COMFORTABLE MIDDLE AGE.

O Sting, where is thy death?

YOUNG MONTAIGNE GOES RIDING

Que scais-je?

I wake up to the sound of music played
on pipes or strings – my father's whim, not mine.
He believes my tender brain might bruise
if I wake too suddenly. Saturnine
cows orbit his estate and confuse
themselves with a grove's piebald shade.

It's early. Bullish nostrils quivering steam.
Dew-shuddering trees and a clatter of stallions.
Stuttering chickens peck and servants scrub
flagstones, an armada of grey galleons
scouring shallows. One of them, a snub-
nosed woman, I recall – that is, I seem

to recall, for I have no memory to speak
of, only curiosity – comes from the same
village on my father's estate where I
was put out to nurse. I greet her by name.
Mornings like these, before the sun gets high,
I like to ride: and I prefer the oblique

paths which wander and meander to the one
which goes straight to the truth. Mist rises
from the fields, all patchwork, like our deeds,
and we ride. How one exercises
one's judgement choosing a suitable steed
is a question worthy of a theologian:

do we judge a horse when racing or at rest
in the stable? And how do we judge a king:
upon the throne of state, or on that private

throne, his private estate? I read the steaming
dollops falling from the jouncing nates
of my companion's horse as I would a text

of some thousands of words, theorising
on the consistency of excrement
and what it tells us of the teeth, the heart,
the firmness of the gut and the contentment
and the clearness of a conscience. The fart
is a different matter: a vapid, rank uprising

disproving the obedience of the anus
as it is discussed in Vives' commentary
on Augustine's man who synchronised
his farting to the steady alimentary
metre of verses that his friends devised.
Usually it is most unruly and mutinous –

much like our current form of government.
I am fortunate to be born in depraved times:
for very little effort I am thought
virtuous; abstaining from the crimes
which are the weapons of that war fought
here, in the hub of civil discontent,

allows me idle hours, time which breeds
chimeras and grotesque things. Variety
alone satisfies me. We pass a field
of sheaves of wheat whispering like a society
of academicians. Weighed down by their yield
they learn humility and lower their heads,

but in the next field ears of wheat rise high
and lofty, heads erect and proud as they
are empty. What do I know? That I can't bear

being shut up in a room, that children play
with knucklebones, men with words, and where,
before they enter our lives, diseases lie

is a mystery? Silent veins of smoke
thread the air. Over the fields a clump
of houses appears, bristling with sound: notes
from a strident rooster, the mill's slow thump.
This is the village where children suckle on goats
and the poor hide their diseases with a cloak

of gentle words which relieve the pain and soften
their harshness. What would we do without names?
Worldly troubles are mostly grammatical
and we have taught our ladies' cheeks to flame
at the mere mention of what they are not at all
afraid to do. Sometimes in daylight. And often.

I could ride for hours: pacing does not tire
me as much as a set journey which forces
me straight ahead instead of the roads which chance
throws up. I think my ideas are like horses.
Sometimes they follow each other at a distance;
at others they glance sidelong at each other.

The path declines and we descend and muddy
hooves spatter our caparisons.
To what could I compare this river? A moulting
snake? What matter our comparisons
when this river, like a civil war, is revolting
against itself, eroding its banks? I study

the surface, shedding scales of light; beneath,
on the river-bed the wind's shadow furrows
its skin like a plough. I study everything:

what I must flee and that which I must follow,
although since my earliest days nothing
has occupied my mind more than death,

but I've never gnawed my nails over Aristotle.
Once, as I stood on the headland of my brother,
the Sieur d'Asac's lands in Médoc, I saw the waves
break over what was once his land. At another
time he had been rich: now, nothing save
fens and drains remain from his battle

with the sea. We continue over dunes
under puffed up clouds and pass a flotilla
of ducks quacking in tiny epicycles
on the current. I cannot stay still. A
mind does nothing but whirl around like little
silkworms which then get tangled in cocoons.

One and the same pace of my horse seems to me
now rough, now easy; the same road at one
time shorter, another time longer; one and the same
view now more, now less pleasing; the sun
now shines too hot, now too feeble a flame
to warm my tired bones. Now I am ready

to do anything, now to do nothing. I do
nothing but come and go and I'm unable
even to rid myself of vice, I just exchange
one for another. Only a fool is immovable
and certain. The sun has become a blazing orange
rising towards the meridian of depthless blue.

It's getting hot. I could stay all day
in the saddle, riding around and about without
flagging. Recently I've heard of a tribe

of cannibals in the new world. I do not doubt
there is more barbarity in eating a man alive
than dead; but who are we to talk, who flay

our enemies alive like dumb creatures
when they are men, like us? These cannibals
know valour; they would rather be killed and eaten
than ask not to be. To a man they are unable
to yield to fear: they are killed, not beaten.
But then again, they do not wear breeches.

A horn sounds. My neighbour hunts again.
Gentlemen are mounting their horses, eager
to course across the grounds and chase some hare,
petrified, and watch lean hounds crush meagre
bones and fur in their grim jaws. I share
the thrill of a hunt, but cannot stand the pain.

I steer my horse homewards – there is a shelf
in my circular library filled with books which say
the earth and planets revolve around the sun.
Perhaps that is the case. For every day
our fortunes change and turn around our sovereign
king. But I revolve within myself.

2002

VELOCITY

A dying man's eyes alive
with the light of television.
Mushrooms, banished by light.
Shadows prop up capped roofs
or fall from gill-ribbed eaves.
A man dying, watching mushrooms,
Swiss browns like ragged penises,
the light of the television flaring
bluishly around his head: a halo
sprouting in the dark, invisible
to his gaze, caught up as it is
with mushrooms. A former boss appears
on the screen in an advertisement
for laxatives. He appears
not to have aged at all, the ex-boss, that is,
although television adds kilos,
subtracts years and scatters spores
of information in the dark.
He's still bald, the ex-boss,
although the man dying is not
that flush with hair either. From underneath
a dirty white toadstool scalp
the ex-boss tries to impose
his authority on people he can't see,
feeding them his image in the dark,
a straw mushroom with no hair
and a dirty beard, bear arms
a little like the prophet Elisha.
On the table is a letter
from another (only just!)
ex-boss, the form guide, the remote.
The man dying alone in the room

no longer feels entirely alone
even though nobody objects to
or remarks on his rapid transformation:
enoki toes, monkey-headed,
two Jews' ears, scaly teeth
and a flicking, russular tongue
and rolling around in his stalk-necked
head, two eyes like black diamonds
scan the screen which scans at twenty-four
frames per second, a single line
from top to bottom flinging
pixels to the four corners of the room.
He is all flesh, a springy cloud
flecked with points of green, red and blue
alone in a room with a television,
a table and on it a box bedded with straw
budding rapid globes, the whites
of upturned eyes. If he lives
long enough, he plans to change
his name: Morel, he thinks, or Mirabeau,
Teonanacatl or possibly Boletus.
He would walk to the registry office
in the shade of his parasol, wearing
a coolie hat, but given the speed
of his decline he must be content instead
to wait for the sudden flare of trumpets,
yellow chanterelles preferably,
which will announce his last vision:
a forest of upstarts burgeons out of nothing,
each trying to overshadow the other.

TEARS

The categories are broken. In their stead
candles blaze and bleed, and a flurry of darkness
chases the light away across the walls.
Faces reappear in the carpet and melt
into animal shapes. Brisk insects maze
the air. The difference between purple and indigo
is about the same as that between occupation
and settlement. Impossible to tell in this light.

Not quite the same is ice afloat on water:
then it's ice or water, even though one
keeps melting into the other, like eyes
filling with water and slipping down a face
into a world which shrinks towards a word
and where, for a while, all boundaries are blurred.

DEATH BY WATER 1: HIPPASOS

...he who first disclosed the knowledge of surds or irrationals and spread it abroad among the common herd perished by drowning...
– PAPPUS, Commentary on Euclid's Elements X

Two
needs
drove him
to his end –
the perfect beauty
of a theorem and, hidden
within, the outrage of its inexpressible truth.

Disagreeing, the retribution they delivered was swift:
between his knowing and their need
for knowledge, he described
overboard
his death's
surd
arc.

DEATH BY WATER 2

It's little wonder I write about water.
Seven generations ago, having shot his load
of rum and sperm in Sydney Cove,
Stephen Tuckerman, Captain of the USS Carolina
disappeared off the coast of Chile with all his crew,
Lieutenant Neil McKellar of the NSW Corps,
despatches from Governor King and the sword
of Captain John Macarthur.
He left behind
an illegitimate son whose daughter,
Mary was widowed in 1856
when her husband, Thomas L'Estrange
drowned while attempting to swim on horseback
across the Cudgegong River then in flood.
The man who tried to rescue him
drowned as well. A raft was built
and eight men were awarded medals
in 1857 *in approval of exertions*
made to recover the bodies of persons drowned.
One of these eight was Harry Albury
whose grandson had Joe Wilson tell
of how he'd *helped drag two bodies*
out of the Cudgegong River in a flood,
and they weren't sleeping beauties.
One hundred
and eight years later Thomas and Mary's grand-daughter
nursed me, her great-grandson in her arms.
That's what happens with death by water:
fiction flows into fact, fact into fiction
and rising up in a flood of words
the past spreads out beyond the present,
carrying into life its drifting dead.

THE BABY BOOMERS

It is the present. The stars are almost as they were, unnameable
constellations imperfectly identified as bears,
a Pontiac convertible, a celtic cross, a seagull
or an albatross, by four friends gazing at attention
from the balcony of a holiday house on a nameless river
near the coast. It's where they've come to stay after the wedding
of some other friends, *joining in early autumn light*
despite the summer heat. Temporary, fragile derricks
pump red oil from their uncovered limbs and then take off,
syrinxing around their ears. The Hunter Valley cabernet
is almost gone; whiffling up from the river, the therapeutic
sound of tiny waves shiatsuing the shore. Property
is the new religion, they are its breathless acolytes;
the cogwheels of their conversation, negatively geared,
are running back towards the day's quiet revolution, sleep.

Morning ploughs the living room through blinds.
They surface like pink bathyspheres and float around the house.
The birds zoom in and out of trees, cicadas fume noise.
Midriffs, thighs, creased earlobes, whiskered jowls: municipally pink.
Grey-timbered trees erupt in vivid, yellow-throated song.
Julie flexes, stretches studiously, sexually important.
Sounds without name move among the forest-floor leaves.
Tinkle of spoons on plates, the slamming fridge, the toaster ballista.
An osprey gathering up the day, lifting it higher, motionless.
After showers patinas of sweat keep on returning.

On stilts: the timber holiday house sounding
the steep escarpment down to the morning riverbank;
flavour walking through their midday meal,
a Julie special, she cannot judge the quantities;
Tony almost walks on water, sagging in the rivermud

as he attempts a circus crossing, a rehearsal
to impress the kids later on; their conversation –
they haven't been together, in a group,
without children for quite some time.
So alcohol's their lantern, over Pictionary®;
inspiration bulbs and dims, invigorates the old
alliances, the new conceits, the rediscovered myths.

Every now and then a thought occurs to them:
the sky is in pieces (it must be something
a witchdoctor said) with nothing in between.
How do they know this? Because they remember
the fitting apart, the falling together
decades ago, which is another country.

Barry lifts the lid on past invention,
the masses' stoichiometry, the city's ravelled streets.
It sort of all coheres, as cold air gathers
underneath the fridge, because it leaks
and cobwebs billow slyly at its back.
There's a recipe for depression,
tailored just for him. How did they know?
His heart is in the right place, so they tell him,
it's his eyes... cross-eyed and clueless
'the people' cheer him on! In an avocado suit
he braves the waves, thinking *what if*
money were see-through? The emperor's new notes?
A thousand gulls are recrudescing on the beach.
Where will it end, the waves' instinctive violence,
the sweep of galactic arms into nothingness?

Debbie lobsters lazily inside all afternoon:
is it super that she's worried about or the complement
of what they do not have? Barry promised everything
and almost got there. Almost: that leaves out gravity,

against which she's been waging war for years. Horizontally,
or lifted by a wave, she's shackled by it and, what's worse,
she knows she's in the wrong, and it is right. That's why she smokes,
she privately admits, that and monumental boredom.

Barry cannot read. He used to, but no longer. His brain
refuses, point-blank, like a mule. He'll put it out to graze
on newsprint, novels, channel-surfing, traffic signs and menus
but it demurs, skips to the end, seeks out the passing cleavage.
He doesn't even read his own reports, they're fiction anyway,
and have a growing readership: he hates the demographic.
From time to time he'll hover over the paper, skimming the stars.

Tony *is* technology, he sometimes thinks aloud,
in the third person. That's why Julie's carnal empire
interests him, he thinks of it as one long line of code:
SetConnect = Julie.CreateObject Connect.Open
        'IntimateConversation'
Intimate.Conversation.SetName = 'Luscious Pie'
Query = "SELECT * FROM Luscious Pie"
Query = Query & "WHERE Mood = 'concupiscent' AND Light = 'Candle'
Option Explicit On
Option Strict On
INSERT into 'Luscious Pie' VALUES 'yes' 'more' 'please' 'again'
Response.Write "aaah"

She can't understand how they have suddenly grown old.
The Julie thing was at its peak when kumera was king,
pesto its prince, sun-dried tomatoes were almost de rigueur,
the currency of chic. Pediments were pastel,
'postmodern' was a seasoning she used to spice her works:
buildings the shade of eyeliner and blush; the neo-, pseudo-
classical porticoes, non-primary colours. And plinths.
Now it's all passé; the flavourings have changed, the money
is the same and she looks young, despite the fact she isn't.

Design is a drug, it cures the future of banality:
that's what she does; her ageing edifices keep her young,
and hungering after clean lines, she architects a world
where holidays are R&D, or so says her accountant.

Debbie lights another gold-tipped cigarette and lies
back on the foam mattress. It's so hot, Barry dissolves
ice cubes in his beer. The sky is bubbling like a spoon
and there's a war in the Gulf. Again. This time they're not sure
whose side they're on or even if there are sides. Tony says
his Volvo has a cold. Imagine that! Girl in Coma
Writes Novel, the radio seems to say, or maybe it's
a line from a Latin American poet without subtitles,
or something like that. Once they used to walk about naked
but an avalanche of flesh means that history now repeats
itself, like that blimp recurring through the palms, saying,
Mozart. Is that a liqueur, Julie wonders, or just a tropical
whatever, himself or cosmic radiation, she's so out of touch.
Even here they are in the suburbs. Who cares about the wedding
cake or the religion hidden between the jokes? Like furry scabs,
flies encrust the drink-rings on the table and a periscope
impales the air. Is it Nemo on the verge of surfacing
or a swizzle-stick out of all perspective? Like tattered underwear,
too many questions hang limply in the air. Cornelius Toad
to Secret Squirrel, are you reading me, over? But Tony's leaning
sideways as he slaloms around a bend and doesn't hear
(Dirtbox Megadeath III, the Final Reckoning) and Barry's off
on a tangent anyway, his chest hurts from reading far too much
about cigarettes or the sublime 'again' in Heidelberg
School light, or maybe it's just Debbie giving him a hard time
about his deafness. When did everyone learn to speak Russian?
Poems lie around the room, stiff as ruined joints.
I was beautiful once, says Julie, *and quite probably sane*.

The river keeps rebooting. An empty crate rebels against
the tide. A yellow scum plaques the river's banks and glides,
like a future thick with disappointment, downstream. The present
has been smoking for some time without any sign
of dissolving into flame. Photographs without colour
pulse on unctuous water. The question is not, 'is it
art?' but how much it is worth, so Barry reckons. An opal
irritated out of clouds, the moon drops into their drinks
and Julie, agape at the stars, starts to get quite sentimental
when she thinks how violently they burn, how long
they've blazed before they all were born and how, despite surviving
them for several billion years, even the stars will die.
Debbie, stalled above a chessboard in her fat bikini,
sarong and sandals, stoops to conquer Barry's white – it's mate.
He's saddened there's no antidote for perfect beauty.
While they go on waiting, Tony's aliens respawn.
Like another 'situation' years ago, they're younger than they think.
He coughs and a cloud begins to weep on Julie, on the deck
a shiny rash appears, becomes a beating film advancing
towards the double doors, and still the children haven't called.

THE WELL

Not choked yet, the well persists
                    in a flurry of unbecoming
leaves and sinews of a baroque
                    vine whose pendant harmonica-
ribbed pods rattle and scrape
                    the shelved neck of river
rocks like lobes hanging heavy
                    with jewellery; surmounting
the mouth a hipped party-hat
                    roof dangles a streamer
bucketed metres down with water.
                    May flies obituarise
themselves in busy lines and summer
                    foretells its own demise
in dense explosions of chlorophyll.
                    Floored by the heat neither
frogs nor pleasure prosper
                    but, busy trapping light,
spiders transform leaves
                    from outside to interior
with a predatory intricate curling.
                    Aiming for the stagnant mirror
of the garden pond the sun
                    misses and instead strikes
the horizon. Mosquitos mass on the border
                    of night and day and launch
their sorties through the heavy
                    lingerie of elephant's
ear, the phosphorescent wake
                    of snails and their faint
fury. Over it all the moon
                    presides in its high black bench,

blind and stern and fattening
                    on what it keeps
for itself, its cold and necessary
                    justice. Otherwise
nights would bleed into sparse dawns
                    and the sun would rise
like a guillotine, only to fall
                    at noon down the deep
pit of the well. Strange, isn't it,
                    how the well is always
full and how the spray of cicada-
                    song leaves you perfectly
dry; stranger, though, is how
                    the bucket, like the pre-
dawn sun, seems to come up
                    before it has risen, ablaze
with subterranean glistening,
                    clearing the snarled throat
of the well with a slight wobble,
                    a slight splash of the new.

BODIES OF WATER

There are not enough words to utter all your fleeting names, O water
– Wisława Szymborska, 'Water'

I've surfed your waves, body-
surfed I mean, surging
through quarrelling foam
onto sand, a polished
twist of driftwood. I've sniffed
your fine capillaries
from where the sky breathes mist
onto mountains, to where
the mountains shrug off creeks,
the closed groin
of valleys veined with them
to backward flowing ripples
on brackish tidal reaches.

I've seen the ocean
and its indifference throwing up
heights and filling in
its restless excavations –
it's a light sleeper.

I've watched your grey clouds
sweat rain, leaf-gilding rain
tossed free with a flick
of the wind, and gyres
of steam rising from summer roads.

And even when I'm taking off,
climbing through your velvet clouds,
slumped in aviophobia,
words, inadequate skyhooks,

go on tethering: torn bread
clouds on a burnished platter,
palm-sweat, drowning eyes,
slow-mo waves below, curling
white window-corner mist,
wing-tips scoring vapour
through the dry heavens,
the horizon's wet blade.

I've seen how, like a dream
that keeps returning
we move from state to state,
water flowing through us,
we through water
a consciousness, a breath.

SEAWEED

Sometimes out of the wet hillocks
a ragged company heaves and settles
in a prickly flush and weave
of beads and beards and weird limbs.

Riddled by fish, the seaweed moves
within itself, a loitering detail
of shredded uniforms and snorkel-stems
swishing towards, away from the beach.

It's only when the sea tips over
in falling walls of white and green
that dark gorillas raise up their arms,
standing up in surrender, or is it praise?

THE EYE

sits on an idea
like a city on its contours,
sharpening lights and slanting shadows.
Inside it lurk dark pockets:
its blind spot clouds the sky.

This city plays the fool; a nasty fool
with loaded fists and sullen flesh
who's hatched an ugly starburst on my face.

The inanely beautiful world goes on:
trees bend and flutter, plums draw the future
into swelling wholes,
taxis graze the streets.
My eye, a hungry nomad,
ranges through the shadow music of the city,
mind-shaded and flat,
cloud-brewed and vengeful,

searching lachrymal corners,
leaving an eye-shaped hole
wherever it lights, hunting
a vision into its socket.

THE OSAGE ORANGE

for Simon West

Winter is blooming
damp, steak-coloured
toadstools and leaves,
papery verso,
purplish fingerprints recto thick on a vine –
a fit gift for a homecoming or calming a house.
Thick humus
ebbs from stone garden walls
and human ornamentals pop up all over the grounds
of Heide's modernism. There's a desert in its sky,
orange leaching westward;
unmoored and floundering
we're like snuff poets
in search of a subject,
wandering about and as uneasy
as if we had found one.

In the gallery inside
monumental art of modern terror
at a safe remove
still cows a little,
depresses a little more
and leaves us bleakened: a version of art which doesn't redeem
but warns or distils: the statue of a judge
looming high over buildings,
only just smaller than the sky,
the broken man on the pier
and the man on the broken pier
or the broken man, running along a disintegrating pier,
wide-eyed and screaming
and in the distance, the size of a mountain,

a ship drifts, menacing
like diplomacy
ancient or modern.

Marmoreal fragments:
the trunk of a lion
caged in glass
is art;
the uncaged lion in the hotel foyer
framed by plate-glass windows is also art;
a sea of wires and girders,
shelled buildings,
Stalingrad chic,
remind us: unfinished wonders are the best art of all.

The unenjoyable game
of the world that wakes at night
and harrows the field of dreams
with foreboding lines
and ready-made scars
fleshes its anxiety with a canniness that bleeds
into the day and almost terrifies,
dissipates
like the experience of recognising your own viscera
burst and shrink in ultrasound
like a wet, clever war.

Outside the wind vowels and thistles
and we walk in the garden,
your skull flowering
black silver ringlets
and you pick up one rotting Osage orange
and then another, pure green and monkey-brained
and turn it over in your hand
as St Jerome might have rolled his skull

around in his hands,
as if its green wrinkles
incarnate a truth
memento mori
memento ludi
unlike the cunning smooth of bone,
a dome convolved with words –
it is a shy brain which fears its subtle folds and what it arranges,
as if it would unbecome itself
be somehow inside-outed,
that something would erupt from it
if it was slammed into the earth
again
and again.

We left them there,
half-shattered and oozing,
damaged wholes
and we drove back to the city
along the scoured gouge of freeway.
Sparsely skewered streetlights flickered on,
and beyond the pecuniary rods and spires,
the west lit up
with a seeping flame,
a faint livid bursting
tipped with orange and gold, a cloud-streaked wort
blossoming there, uncurled and lingering, almost whole.

PORT HACKING, SOUTH-WEST ARM

Commanding knowledge greater than the pin-pricks
of its eyes allow, neck erect, Egyptian-like
and ruddering strongly in a straight line,
undercutting the ever-changing dimpled peaks,
the salt-oil brimmings and shallowings,
the slender snake crosses the south-west arm
of the port, already in full possession of the other side.

UNCOLLECTED

BEES

They came into her studio,
singly through the vandal-

shattered pane. The first one stayed
her brush-stroke, a tenor viol's

urgent open C, then others, pitched
at lower keys, small radios

buzzing static, then more until
she was afraid. They bearded half an easel

with a dirty flame, popping live coals
that fizzed among the canvases. Her husband patched

the broken window, filled the room with spray
then left it locked. And waited. Two days later,

crisp beneath their sandals:
a lawn of tiny dead, like twists of tracing paper.

That night, she woke in this dream:
between her legs, an avid swarm.

WOLLOMOMBI FALLS

Vertigo begins in the groin:
which is why space carries on below us
in empty strides, we the umbilical
astronauts tumbling up in blue.
From the bottom of the gorge, a thin roar
of falling water tempts us with the knowledge
you can fall only once.

The fence resists temptation: it's a scar
of woven metal. Some birds descant
from open beaks above the plunging silence.
The trees are tentative, leaking wind:
I remember balancing on the edge
of puberty and thinking, the future sprouts
from scars like these. A mirror

flings a present at the future.
Something as rare as forgiveness in scrabble
happens from time to time: twenty, thirty
years ago a dog fell down this gorge
and survived with only a broken leg.
I think about survival, like the chartreuse-
coloured lichen on the northern side of tree trunks:

I'd thought myself immune to the sublime
having bounced off a tightrope once and survived.

FROM *CONCRETE TUESDAY* (2011)

RIPPLES

What is the number of water?
As many as the ripples going nowhere
across the surface of the pond.

I've counted them in my ear
and on my fingers. Scanned by wind,
they rise out of nothing,

roofing the pool with see-through tiles
that slide away from where
they were, from where the action was

to where they go: a steady ticking
off into nothing, cool sines
fluttering the axis at the pool's lip.

Every now and then the air
damages the water with graphs
of gooseflesh, but then the liquid grooves

resume their count, marching lines
that rise and dip:
as many as I am and more, much more.

FOG

Moving house is a myth:
the old floor plan and worn
curtains leaning in
on the dwindled labyrinth

are the same as before, stacked
T-wise in their shelves, books,
a brass crocodile, rocks
and postcards, a rubber duck

memorialising glorious failures
on the cricket field: all unchanged,
Titanic deckchairs rearranged.
Stunning windows, fog

lures me outside and stumps trees,
prunes headlights, dampens
everything in woollen
silence. The earth lurches

into unknowing and I'm
beside myself, thrilled
with the thin new swirl
up steps, the worm-wheel climb

to nothing. But one myth
interrupts another, the cradle
of these words, a candle
stammering in the wet breath

of morning, the telling of it.
Nothing doesn't last,

the first and oldest
truth or myth, it hits

me right between the eyes
every time. That's why
hours after the sky
had rolled its blue eyes

I was inside, at the edge
of the chopping board staring
at a squeezed lemon wedge:
yellow prawn legs dangling.

WET SEASON

That is no country for old men

1.

The air begins where bodies end,
thick with insects. Shoes and belts
bloom green powder. People drink
at the wet atmosphere,
yeasty squalls and tongue-pokes
of rain, the year's tantrum.
Where red mud sinks
everything into itself, cavernous
clouds as vast as corporations
plump the atmosphere, churning towers
split with cold lightning.
Crowded around the light-bulb,
a gossip of flying things.
Gossamers drift lankly from transoms.

2.

The giant tanker lords the window
with skyscraper metal, impossible
that it will miss the classroom
thick with lassitude but does,
swerving mid-channel, deck eye-level
and prow sheering up the port.
The ore express rattles through the lesson,
the shortest distance between two points itself.
The iron ship equals the hole in the earth
plus the carriage-loads stuffed down its maw.
Between the clouds and earth
remains a bucketing chasm
where bodies drip from themselves
and birds release their song.

3.
Nothing can be written:
paper softens, wilts.

What is written smudges
in blurry heat: the names and numbers,

the artifice of power.
The children learn drowsily,

then explode outside their class,
climbing crushed cliffs

and steep cones of ore,
staining themselves with muddy blood.

Shifting the mountain only takes a lifetime.
The double-entered books mirror

the silting port
they will keep on dredging.

READING LAURIE DUGGAN IN THE SHANGHAI NEW ZHEN JIANG RESTAURANT

If only I spoke Mandarin
like a peasant, I'd say to the waiter
who compliments my crap Hanzi
copy of the restaurant name, I *could do better*
if only I had prepared
(great deathbed confessions: if only...).
I'd take my time,
learning how to speak like a child
and not pretend. Great translations
take gall and humility in equal measure.
I feel like putting up my hand
and asking for an extension
or another serving of the eggplant dish.
Meanwhile, Laurie is hacking into Les again;
downstairs, a banshee scream
of a little emperor thwarted.
It's death, my aunt says, and he's
reading your poems.
Frank Sinatra sings 'Unforgettable'.

THE POET'S HOUSE

Tal vez ésta es la casa en que viví
cuando yo no existí ni había tierra
– Pablo Neruda, *Casa*

1. Conservatory

Quiet please. A flower unfolding from the end of her arm,
her hand bequeaths meaning to the room: his reading chair,

a gift from T— (at the end of each arm a martini
holder); between the mirrors on the wall bloom signed

Mapplethorpes; smelling of decaying flesh, joints
of orchid fingers grasp the air. *He never worked in here*

but read or let the harbour swell above the balcony
and flood his mind. That's when the group release a symphony

of admiring gasps. It's a quote! *The Rydalmere*
Sonnets, breathes one; too early, smiles another – it's *The Point*

Piper Pyrrhics. She's been murmuring all afternoon, this guide,
and flashing choice exhibits, a little like a porn queen. He

would have approved too, pervert that he was, aware
of the seamy in the sublime. He never meant any harm

2. Library

but managed plenty anyway. *Fifteen thousand volumes*
in three rooms, six languages including Swahili

and first editions signed by friends – he needed no index
'save his insecurity', he said. See there? The shelves

are column graphs plotting his career: a hundred spines
all straighter than his own, the selected and collected in

translations: it's a library within a library. *That's where*
his third wife died when the set of shelves collapsed. They say he found her

four days later, returning from a festival in Dunedin.
Decomposition had already set in. That's how the lines

about his ego as a weapon came about, 'my many selves
all bent on death / my words are love's destruction / this desk

where I have authored hell.' They've heard it all before, but still the
group tut-tuts in sympathy and *oh dears* fill the rooms.

3. Sunroom

They walk along a corridor, the sunroom, lined with photographs
of poets, his private pantheon: the fiercely bulbous Baudelaire,

Merrill's boyish grin and Bishop's bun, her gaze slanting
down to the marina, a grove of gently tilting masts;

next, Slessor elegantly naphtha-flashed, a uniformed Apollinaire
and the older Yeats, pince-nez, eyes closed, head thrown back, chanting.

But after Moore and bird-beaked Mandelstam, finely dusted
with golden light, a silver gelatin emulsion

mottled in a corner with the kind of caramel blisters
a portrait edged into a flame might have, the odd one out:

not one, but three poets, a photo taken somewhere in the out-
back. The man is T—, flanked by two women, evidently sisters,

one of whom stares at the lens with a look of near-revulsion –
the poet's second wife – the other with her bosom squarely thrust at

4. Dining Room

T—, who smirks happily. *The dining room*, their guide declares,
as if it wasn't obvious: a narrow room dominated

by a nautical theme; made from recycled railway sleepers,
the captain's table and thirteen chairs. *Perhaps his greatest passion*

after poetry and, I suppose, his wives, was dinner parties.
He loved to dress up and surprise his guests from this trapdoor,

and right on cue an acned youth in pirate costume *ta-dah's*
out through a panel in the wall. *Thank you Gavin*, and pairs

of wrinkled hands flap lightly in applause. They're a tad deflated
by the theme park feel: what they really want is to weep as

they're told stories of his tragic genius, his possession
by a force greater than himself – but the rhetoric of the heart is

nothing compared to that of the spleen. *For guests that he abhorred,*
mainly critics, there's a trapdoor underneath some chairs.

5. Kitchen

They turn into the tiled chamber he called 'my private chapel'.
An altar, once piled high with offerings stands in the centre, cowled

by a metal hood; four burners of unequal size gleaming
on a bed of stainless steel; next to them a spouted tower

of olive oil, garlanded with garlic. *He said that cooking*
was a form of poetry: 'Like rhymes, /the flavours of a dish /

chime musically against my palate./The poetry of food
is tuned / to the fulfillment of a wish,/baked apple

consummates the pork, / a knife desires its fork /and cold
desserts blaze with an orange liqueur. She gazes as if dreaming,

so she says, of mascarpone and tinned peaches with sour
cherries (her favourite). They had come into this room looking

for art, unalloyed, but have found instead an appetite: Quiche
Lorraine is on one mind, Chicken Tikka another and the stewed

6. Garden

peaches have made their tummies gurgle noisily with hunger.
Just as well: the mid-point of their tour sees them all led

outside, down a mosaic path skirting the dark ferns
to a small café in the garden. Aproned this time, Gavin returns

to take their orders – today's specials being the Dante Salad,
Omelette à la T—, the Yeats Burger, Kangaroo Bangers

and Mash (drizzled with truffle oil). And it's pleasant enough,
even if a little pricey. From where they sit, the house's

underparts are visible, looming blackly on the rise
above them like a dark wood with trees of pale stone.

Those near the guide are lucky enough to hear in an undertone
the story of his first wife: how she supervised

the building of the house, wore the trousers,
bankrolled him – did everything but leave him well off

7. Basement

when she left him for that female architect from Rome.
How he must have suffered, someone sniffs, while another rambles

on about 'artistic types' they're so, you know, *bohemian*,
and they'd go on except with all that coffee, the glass of wine –

somewhere in the basement they will find his favourite room
still in operation and restored to the shambles

he preferred. Someone whispers, *What's a mise en abyme, Ian?*
but Ian didn't get it either; besides, he's watching the line

forming outside the dunny coil out into afternoon
light. It barely moves. Each occupant leafs through the jumble

of books and journals – it's T—, all T— or so it seems. An
etching of T— is thumb-tacked to the back of the door under *Vaseline:*

an Ode, the only thing of his in the room. What they don't know:
he died of a stroke while on that throne, fifteen years ago.

8. Spiral Staircase / Gallery

Around the corner, bolted to the concrete floor, a spiral
metal staircase screws the middle of the house,

leading first to an enclosed terrace
overlooking the garden. Painted on the far wall, a mural

by his fourth wife, the environmental activist, a moral
fable of rapacity, the squander and abuse

of non-renewable resources. *No one could accuse*
him of lacking a sense of irony, however cruel,

she says and fans her fingers over a glass case full of coral,
one of many natural wonders plundered from the seas,

the beaches, rivers, forests, deserts... in all, a dozen cases
filled with rare specimens: the spiral tusk of a narwhal

next to Midas slit shells, swordfish swords, a Colophon
stag beetle lording it over the hornworm sphinx moth. On

9. Theatrette

one side wall, Parnassians transfixed by mounting pins;
on the other, Pilbara olive python and anaconda skins.

When he became ambassador-at-large for Australian
culture he toured the world religiously ransacking alien

countrysides (when not making those ridiculous
advertisements for television), sending these enormous

containers home crammed full with dead endangered flora, fauna —
it was too much for his fourth wife: they found her dead in a Korean sauna,

an overdose, apparently. She leads them through a green
door into a theatre with less than a dozen seats, a screen,

projector and, at the back, a well-stocked bar. *He liked to show*
home movies here, or drink. Or both. No one really knows

what the movies were about – they're said to feature T—
and the second wife. If she has them still, they're under lock and key

10. Study 1

in the other house, where she still lives, in Byron Bay.
How disappointed they all are! Those DVDs they saw

for sale downstairs are not the fabled flicks on Super 8,
but documentaries, himself reading... Their helical

ascent resumes, half a twist onward into the room where it all
happened. *He called this room the minefield, where he'd 'detonate*

words, / sweep verbal seas for meaning.' He worked in here from four-
thirty in the morning until noon, every day.

It doesn't seem the kind of room a great poet would write in:
unfurnished floors, bare walls, no books, a window with no view

save of the back garden and a desk to match his *mulga-*
jointed fingers / suited more to laying bricks than / vulgar

words in transcendental patterns. On the desk are two
sheets of paper, the uncompleted poem he was writing

11. Study 2

when he died, titled simply 'T—', even though
T— had predeceased him by some twenty-odd years.

The first line starts: *He wrote as slowly as a continent /*
drifts, millimetring towards greatness / He wrote like a dog /

pissing against posts, marking out his territory /
He wrote as if he had the soul he lacked, / plumbed depths

that had not been before he wrote / He wrote like a potato /
sprouting eyes while shriveling / He always wrote in arrears, /

pursued by avid creditors, but always making payment,/
He wrote just like himself, and there it stops: the catalogue

just peters out, even though it seems that there's a story
to be told, of him and T—. Everyone accepts

he is the stronger poet now, whereas early death for T—
(and a good-looking corpse) at the time meant immortality,

12. Bathroom

which nearly drove him mad: relative longevity
was all that he'd allow his rival's work, and therefore his own.

It takes a while for all of them to read the poem; some
of the oldies have to lean right over, peering over their glasses

at the great man's scrawl. Then they dawdle out and bunch outside
the only room that can only be locked from inside. *When creativity*

deserted him, he came in here, took off the dressing-gown
in which he wrote and showered until the next line would come.

And if it didn't, he wasn't fussy: any old catharsis
would do, if it unblocked him. The bathroom is rather outsized,

and her voice attacks the tiles like a fifties singing star,
all zing and reverb bouncing off the porcelain, mirrors and chrome.

They remain in the hall, she inside, even though there's enough room
in there for swinging a small leopard (there's a three-seater spa,

13. Master Bedroom

a claw-footed tub awash with a flush of yellow rubber ducks,
a balcony, ceiling to floor mirrors): it feels like an intrusion

even now, on the great man's private space. *Next door's the Master*
Bedroom and a guest room, she says, leading them on, *he never*

had any children. The rooms are left the way they were when he died.
They gather by a river of rippled folds lapping at the edges

of a king-sized bed which, when he was younger, coursed nightly
with torrents of flesh. Above it, hanging on the wall, a Whitely

nude, all pear-shaped arse and harbour views. The guide stretches
up and takes it down to reveal a small hole through which he spied

sometimes on guests, those younger couples he invited whenever
he needed to remember what desire was, snout to plaster,

in his later years. *It's said his second wife left him when, in collusion*
with T—, he watched him with her sister. She walked in on the efflux

14. Observatory

of his clandestine surveillance, clocked him with a vase
then left. It shattered him. He wrote of her, 'She was the tonic /

to my soul's gin' and after losing her for good to T—
he lost the plot entirely: he drank, and then began construction

of the tower we are climbing now. She puffs a bit,
having talked so much, leading them up the spiral way.

She's older than they thought, they think, as one by one they crowd
into the round summit. The rising moon is masked by a cloud

passing blackly across it. It's dark. It is the end of their day.
Street lights blink into life. A telescope pokes out through a slit

in the glass dome roof. *During that time, bent on self-destruction*
he'd spend his nights up here. He'd use the telescope to see

into those houses. It was only later, in his hydroponic
phase that he found the love that moves the sun and other stars.

AUTOAKHOTIC

1.
Driving in rain near Cooma
from nowhere to nowhere
along a twist in the mind or road,
dense gums straight and allusional
and behind them, cloud-mountains
and their scree of rain,
softening into a furze of grey animosity:
nothing helps me here,
my own fading witness,
nor you, not knowing where you are.

2.
Morning light is feeding off the freeway
and I am peeling back kilometres
more like a banana than an onion.
All along the roadside, morning trees
chop down light
and shadows thrum the passing cars
as your voice strums my memory
and slipping in and out of darkness,
your face, obscured by hair, incomplete.

3.
Grief and driving fit together
like a tongue to teeth:
searching for the street I don't know,
failing, always ending up near home.

I light the language-fuse with grief,
your death, these words
the way home. But why not silence,
blunted streets and voiceless breath?

I accidentally threw this poem out,
but where you are and where I am
are not so very far apart now.
And so you found me here, again.

MACHINE CODE

My eyes are like machine code, running lines
up from the lanes and screens
or avenues of trees my limbs walk down,
which open up my mouth or make me squint.
It's one thing to think about it,
another thing to live it through,
when resemblances cannot be told apart
from repetition. Bubbles wobble and rise
from a morning dive in the pool
where after several laps I tire and lose count.
If comparisons were true instead of pathways,
fishing lines, I'd happily shut down
but it's not the truth that wakes me up at 3am,
just its piercing semblance.

CONCRETE TUESDAY

happens only in winter, beginning in a narrow street
in orphaning light
where cars shrink into their parking spaces,
nosing each other like dogs,
under a sky without colour, damp and clear. From dirty holes
in the bitumen, bare veins thrust into the sky,
devoid of leaves. Up and down the street the sound of doors
snapping shut, the sounds of hunkering down, of rattling blinds,
the shiver of keys, terraces diminishing into themselves,
and I realise this is the kind of day where I know
what it's like to be part of a species,
a day that doesn't belong to me, but to animals and their ignorant thrall
to DNA, ours and theirs, to the fear in rustling leaves
as my shadow passes them, to cancer and IVF,
to fucking in the cold weltering moon
of a bedside lamp and finding in shadows
the face of a lost or forgotten loved one,
to bronchioles opening and choking, to the fug of sleep
and the gritty, uncovering dawn, to the plucking of dew
and the slow gather of fog, and the gutters of fast trickling,
to a bole with its half-moons of amputation,
to a statue of father, mother and child, moss-stained
and faceless, to the fluorescent burrows
in which we excel and word, to running and to the flight
of cat's eyes as the lane changers hone their art,
to cigarettes, to the minarets of absolute capital.
On this day, people are like cars, on high beam
and nudging each other and passing, ragefully,
low clouds dwarfing the personal,
clouds low in the sky's brow creased in conversation,
all the colours of the day chosen from a palette
of reticent tones and shades.

It's a day I negotiate. As one does a hillside
or a contract, each as slippery as the other,
and dealt with as with a minor catastrophe,
not the sort that leaves knuckles red from wringing
or memory cauterised, but is like the slow collapse
of habitual happiness into something more provisional,
into a set of ideas which can't be classified
or extraordinary states of mind unshared
except in retrospect, in the way that each generation
finds the music of its successors alien,
a set of special horizons in which we zoom about,
bucking against the statistics and confirming them.
The gutters peeping rain seem almost spontaneous.
On such a day as this I wish I were following someone,
a man or a woman, it doesn't matter which,
and he or she is wearing a suit
of mirrors which throw off prodigiously the details of the day:
the city and its incisions, barbaric and cultured,
no choice but no choice, only consequent actions,
walking with gusto and throwing the world back at itself,
the world cut up into parts, becoming the ultimate fashion accessory,
drawing a crowd who would follow the mirrors
up the rancid lane where next to the butts and syringes,
a sign is chalked on a piece of plywood
that looks like a ripped-out heart, saying
'Concrete Tuesday' and an arrow which,
as it happens, is pointing straight at me.

GRACE

The Queen: 'It's a poor sort of memory that only works backward'
– Lewis Carroll, *Through the Looking Glass*

Retribution. A demon, a hideous shape
receding across the wheat-filled plain.
A dark flurry at the edge of the forest.
My eyes opened to a page
of fine print, an open book page-down
and covering my face like a gas mask
or alien larva. Swimming back,
my eyes began to focus on some words,
. . . fail shall they, prophecies, et cetera, but the book
fluttered shut as I placed it on the floor.

I got out of bed and switched off the lamp
on the bedside table. The mozzie zapper steamed,
odourless in the dark. I was wide awake.
My wife lay snoring softly in the bed.
I vomited clear water into a glass.
On the television a gangster took his gun
out of the mouth of his victim, holstered it
and retreated back down the stairs.
Outside, everything was dark:
an empty bus reversed slowly up the road.

I had no memory of the day before.
The new day pulled me on, like a magnet
trawled through a garbage tip, to dawn.
I attracted a cab without flagging it down
and it took me to a diner I knew, still serving
dinner, not yet breakfast. I wasn't hungry.
What's more, I threw up into an empty bowl.
It looked like carrots and macaroni:

minestrone, in fact, but it still smelt like spew.
A scowling waitress came and took it away.

I wandered around the city, not really looking
where I was going, and ended up at the casino.
Business must have been bad. Doormen were picking
drunks up off the footpath and hauling them in
like cattle into an abattoir. A peeled hard-boiled
egg flew out of the darkness and into my hand.
It was miraculously whole, so clean
I could have eaten it. And I was tempted.
But the more I gazed at it the more I thought
it belonged to another. That's when I saw Robert de Niro

or his double waving from a crowd of people breaking
into a basement bar. I approached him, quaking
in my boots. We shook hands as if we were friends,
went down and in and picked up some empty glasses
and started drivelling into them like all the rest,
gulping down nonsense and laughter. The lights dimmed
and brassy voices blared and tinkling cymbals
of laughter echoed off the mirrors and walls.
De Niro was saying something about an Otto
as if I knew him, Otto this and Otto that,

and his face creased as he spoke in a worried V.
I started to look around in case this Otto
was there. How would I recognise him? Trouble
always looks for trouble. That's when I noticed
the crowd. They were international A-list,
or so I thought (I might have been seeing double).
I saw Cameron Diaz, who saw me with stuttering eyes
and Russell Crowe, who was raucously blotto.
Our Nicole slapped Bill Clinton and, behind them,
echelons of risen dead luminaries

gathering darkly in chatter. A pair of Oscar Wildes
were reproaching a painting, or was it the wallpaper?
I was too far away to hear. On stage were some Beatles:
She Said, She Said, I heard John Lennon sing,
but the rest of the lyrics were lost in the din.
I overhead Hitler complaining of haemorrhoids,
for which Ché Guevara recommended a cure
of shark's egg soup and potatoes. In a corner
a handful of popes and a few pied pipers
were passing a number around. It was getting wild.

The walls of the joint were convict-chiselled
and the bar was like a crypt, it even had pews.
Princess Di reclined on one – Marlon Brando
was feeding her grapes. On another was Bon Scott
and Margaret Scott comparing family trees.
I looked up and out through a grated window
and watched as a shark-shaped cloud swallowed
the moon. That's when I heard the applause,
the whistles and shouts as the room went numb
with Madonna and Marilyn Monroe, semi-

nude, descending the stairs. They waved
and turned every now and then to show off
their frill-knickered butts. For this was charity,
not knowing in part, but in full. From their garters
they stuffed into hands and flung in the air
banknotes, spinning around all the while like Hills Hoists,
gathering clothes as they went. They disappeared
fully clothed, and even though we shouldn't need it,
we were all richer for it. I had a moment of clarity:
If I didn't know my past, I loved my future.

I started to drink less quickly, sobering up,
and gave my egg to De Niro. I told him
I'd only eat it. We left together, yakking
all the way under a yolk-stained sky
towards a hotel. For some reason I called him Paul.
He gave me a roll of cash. I wasn't lacking,
I said, but he said nothing and left.
The wad tingled in my pocket and drew me
into the lobby, into a lift and (I didn't dream
this up) into a suite as wide and roomy

as heaven. On the bed was a naked woman,
weeping. She looked a little like Cameron Diaz.
My suit disappeared and I found myself
hunkered above her. Before I knew it
I was inside her and coming, but I kept on at it,
the tears had stopped, no kissing, just the surf
of desire building until I eventually stopped,
rock-hard and weeping. By the end of it all
she was looking more like herself, Diaz
I mean, lollipop eyes and a mouth as wide

as the Harbour Bridge. Without so much as a word,
so muddy with desire, I knocked on the door
as I left, a kind of tattoo, I guess, saying *thanks*
for the screw, ooroo and I was off on my career
across, or was it downtown? God alone knew where.
In Martin Place I passed a bloke dabbing tears
on his cheeks and drawing a crowd. In Elizabeth
I saw a tired old man slumped on the footpath
who revived a little at seeing me, his breath
hissing into him slowly. And I saw how hope

was like a drug creeping back into his veins,
his hand on his heart as he looked up in surprise

as I gave him back his past. I stuffed his empty hat
with cash as he snarled and wailed and tried to grab
my hand in gratitude. I left him whimpering,
overwhelmed by the restoration of his faith
in humanity. He could have been my father.
It seemed I was heading towards the Cross.
Dry leaves snuffled about in the wind. A wolf
dressed in a bonnet drove by on the side of a bus.

Before too long I was standing outside a tower,
filled with a mighty potency and magnificence.
I ascended through the core like an embolism,
emerged into a boardroom's sheen and assumed
my rightful place at the head of the table.
As timid as scholars the board filed in
not daring to face me until they had bowed
into their seats and raised their hands in salute
or assent. They had agreed to share my share
in the company, delivering them from improvidence,

and freeing me at last from worldly cares.
For at last I had earned the truth: I was a god.
I had no need to look before I leapt,
my chickens had all been counted before they'd hatched
from a single basket of eggs made into an omelette
I'd given to Peter and called the tune – the future
couldn't hurt me because it's the past of the present,
sweetened by a rose. I spoke three words
and the board backed out of the room without their eyes
leaving my face, all except my accountant,

Richard Merkin (I'm telling this how it was)
who smiled at me with teeth like rows of zeros
and took me to lunch at Piffellini's. A real piece,
this Merkin, all laptop and bottom line,

drawing money out of my accounts over wine
and barely touched plates of pasta, which some capers
and salmon had walked through on stilts. We drooled
our way through lunch, I barely puked, and what I did
was whole and clean. My signature leaked from some papers
up into my pen. Then the world sped up and overtook me.

This is where it gets dark and I cannot connect
the dots. I arrived in the city's old testament,
the quarter of blood and terror. The earth surrendered
a leaping man, who acquired the top of a tower
by his thumbs. I approached a warehouse. Rats waddled
towards me, brandishing tails. Open drums gulped smoke.
Inside was a man playing patience, scooping up cards
like leaves, a Popeye tattoo on his bulging bicep
complete with corncob pipe, Malcolm Turnbull
jaw and emblazoned across his arm, the motto:

I yam what I yam. I was face to face with Otto,
I guessed. I gave him a sheet of paper, numbers
and words and we walked past a small television
showing the 4th Global Lookalike Convention
and into a vast open space where human hoovers
on hands and knees went around sucking up blood
from the concrete floor. It couldn't have been their own.
When they finished, some other guys patted them down,
roughly at times, but there wasn't a bruise or a scratch.
We must have had a bet or a deal: Otto gave me a scroll

of lobsters bound by a tight rubber band.
He pointed out Cameron and noted her beauty,
how she closely resembled the truth. Disappearing
into his finger was her name. He gave me a coat
and shook my hand saying, Otto Sharkey or something
like that. A joke? Some of the men snickered,

some simpered. I no longer knew the difference
between laughter and crying. *You see too nice*, said Otto
and I was out in what seemed like a light rain
falling up, then in a cab with the sky turning silver.

Dogs hushed their barking as I hoofed the gate open at home.
Always to be pitied, a human alone. I was dead
on my feet. It was only just sunset – no *Law & Order*
for me, just white noise thoughts: one man's laughter
is another manslaughter. I creaked into bed
beside my wife who was stretching asleep
and closed my eyes on a wheat-filled plain.
A white horse was galloping through it
towards me, ever so slowly. Sunlight disappeared
into a white-hot hole in the sky, full of grace.

CODICIL

…and after my body has been released from the morgue
I will have my head removed, the skull cleaned
and a transverse section made from brow to just under crown,
rough bony edges sanded smooth and varnished,
perhaps, to be gentle on the lips and tongue,
and then onto the hippocampus, the supraspinal fossa
and onto the pan of the frontal and parietal lobes
I will have an alloy of silver and gold poured,
like an inland sea teeming with dull reflections,
seeking the lower depths and cooling
into a moulding of that osseous seat of fear
and pleasure; and then, once the metal has cooled,
I will have the first of the wine poured into it,
a shiraz or a pinot noir, and then the skull shall be passed
from hand to hand, and with each draught taken from it,
loosened tongues will make of my name an oath or an execration.

2012–2020

FROM *ANATOMY OF VOICE* (2016)

THE FIRST PARTITION

host guest ghost

Somewhere a voice
near my mind not in it
but part of it apart
and tethered by memory

comes to me I am drawn
to its foiling surface
sleeved with sense its limb
of sound And it fills me with grief

It is the voice of someone
dead but it lives on
somewhere between my mind
and the vast-roomed night

sleeve self false

Colours arrive with song
cold calling birds
throating the dawn the dew
rising slowly as lives begin

and end voices ignite
putter about and mesh
the radio voice invisible
suturing at a distance

minds to bodies fact
to feeling this muscle of sound
flexes noise into knowing
fastens the silence with selves

I take with me into the day
this thing I half-remember
half-create   a dry fire
dissolved in my blood

as smooth as knives the flights
of two birds twin and peel
apart   in a fluid line
threading the trees

and foresting the great unquiet
with song   your voice
gutters on   so far from home
                              at home

Into the labyrinth of language
in search of a body   you
find me in my dreams
Your voice   deaf

can only speak   unfolding silence
Away from itself it burrows
into the mind's ear
into its finials   rounding the void

with its skull of words
closing around the fontanelle
of darkness   Give me an ear
and I will show you a voice

What does it weigh?   your voice?
Less than a book?
As much as a life?
Mountains range the horizon

but the desert keeps on growing
vast as language
and the one crying out in it
is alone and forever

Thought in the mouth
the myth of thinking
apart from voice shatters
it comes from another   within

After the word the worm
and after flesh loam
and after dark earth rolls
in its clammy grasp bones

there is only voice the snag
of word in memory
the mind's home
made bright with words

Sunrods host
the falling dust motes
in this house of many rooms
its threshold made of voice

hone honest throne

I follow your voice down its path
and although its words are not
'follow' or 'obey'   I follow and obey
and come into a subtle world

where the distinctions are fine
as blades of grass or leaves on trees
where firewood is not firewood
and the sun spins a web of light

through floating trees and shivering limbs
and the vine which persists through the dead ones
This is the ungarden   the maze of spring
the flowers which have their root in your voice

The city is silting up
with voices   incessant light
and things in leather   streets are slits
of speed   mirroring the uncity

translating stars into chatter
night into smooth panes
when the city quietens
to a ravenous hum

gathers its intervals
shells the silence
in a desert of neon
Darkness crowds the stars

THE FOURTH PARTITION

Out of the depths I cry to you, O Lord, hear my voice!

Psalm 130

I think of you in my car
driving through forest where trees chop down sunlight

and the bush is alive with the sound of machinery
the chirruping of mobile phones

driving through forest in stuttering light
weaving through roadkill and veering

with the road, the way which separates
land from the time of travelling

I think of you in this liminal hour
the worlds we inhabit touching

at this single point, this trace
of a wound which does not scar

on the boundaries of our selves
always arriving, that which calls

across heavens, from room to room,
joining us through air, through love

and dividing us from silence
this gift of the next-to-nothing

that we carry in our mind's heart
the voice of a siren at its purest, silent

conjuring nothing out of something
the void which goes on voicing in the dark

I think of you driving through forest at sunset
the sun runs its stick of light against a fence of trees

FROM *NUMB & NUMBER* (2019)

COASTLINE

I walked along the cliff-top at around eleven
one September morning, wondering why the level
of the sea at the horizon
seems always higher than where I am, even though
the waves kept shuddering into spray on rocks far below.

Was it a kind of horizontal vertigo,
or a species of the sublime, a newly released *cogito*,
I think therefore... I must be a dwarf
standing on the shoulders of other dwarves, each one shorter
than the one before? I filed this thought for

later use and kept walking past clumps of hustling
grass, on a concrete path glittering in bright sunlight,
past a jogger threshing air,
all elbows, knees and sweat, who paused a moment, oinked,
or so it seemed, and jogged on. The morning light coined

a mint of silver on the ocean, golden shivers
of droughty stalks flared from the footpath's fissures
and I was rich for a moment,
richer than the waterfront exclusionary
viewkeepers, the prinked promenaders, even the cemetery.

I passed a clique of tourists gathered at a corner
of the white retaining fence, where locals reckon
the face of the Virgin Mary
appears each day at around eleven, and armed with cameras
and mobile phones they waited with a calm air as

if faith was merely a matter of patience. I prepared
to wait for a while as well, but nothing appeared
to happen, so I strolled on, dissatisfied
as ever. Back then I wanted to be an anagram
of what I should have been: not a Manager,

but a flâneur perhaps, or a traveller or taghairm
prophesying in ox-hide by a stream, or migrate
in reverse to my two great-
grandfathers, Musgrave and Quealy, who lived across the Shannon
from each other but never knew it, sang their Hosannas

to different Gods and croaked here only eighty miles
and twenty years apart. Would I assimilate
or be assimilated there,
an exile in a land of unfamiliar rain,
a thonged exotic flaw in emerald terrain?

No theme comes from exile except exile, something
no one bothered to tell the ex-pat generation.
Until now, I thought.
I watched some yachts puff south like beery slobs, all gut
and no behind. A seagull carried on like a galoot

above my head and then the path began declining
into oblongs balkanized by weed-cracks, kindling
memories of jigsaws:
fitting patiently on wet Sundays piece to piece,
sifting through the pile for the opposite

of a promontory of cloud: portly swastikas,
running men, whimsies, wheat sacks,
Swedens, Sulawesis, bits
of continent or a cauliflowered florescence, Mandelbrots
ferning into shapes running through my bloodstream.

And then the bigger pieces: the absent shape of you
to which no piece will fit, like emptied rooms
in a house no longer habitable.
Loss ineluctable: there is no cure, no magic zebra
crossing to a lossless world. Aslant in the breeze

I walked the cliff-top walk, totally alone
at the other end of love, on the way from one littoral
to another, balancing an act
in a world out of balance, piecing together words
to confront something, long ago put to the sword.

Level with my eyes a seagull hovered, motionless
into the wind. I passed beer cans in modern middens,
dandelions on the path's port side
while slowly from the north-east, thunderheads of mackerel-
mottled clouds began to coolly spit on the caramel-

coloured cliffs. It's funny how it worms
its way in, love, diasporated like a swarm
of angry bees bearding a heart.
The continents are the oldest divorcees, having drifted
apart for eons. Next to them we've barely tiffed.

But still you reappear, even if only as a pronoun
which has to be emptied out or not pronounced
as once it was: as you.
Almost anyone could be one of them,
an economy of love which we won't fathom.

You can stand for anyone now, there is no end:
the reader of this poem or the one you need
as elementally as air.
And so I kept on walking, finding in a word the future
and the past in ever-repeating series bearing a kind of fruit

into the present. And as I walked, I came to resemble Achilles
racing the tortoise, never overcoming, in the end, a calculus
of ever decreasing lengths.
But I wasn't frustrated – *au contraire* – I was fascinated:
for love, like every coastline, properly considered, is infinite.

2012

THE MANUSCRIPT

As he watched the last of the manuscript curl into ash
he followed her footsteps of years ago
past the blue metal swathe of rail,
down narrow acacia, callistemon streets
towards the silos and scrap metal merchants,
through the underpass that resembled a public urinal
with its stench, mossy drippings and gridded lights
to the bachelor flat at the rear of a house that groaned and shuddered
with each passing train, imagined as he found it to be, years later,
a gas spigot beaking one corner, a cobwebbed window looking over
a concrete backyard, little more than a bed and kitchenette
disappearing into ionised air, he realised
he'd stubbed out the last of a stubborn obsession, but not the story
of how, night after night, she'd traverse the restless suburb
then after each assignation return through the urinous underpass,
up the narrow acacia, callistemon streets to the share house
where her daughter was baby-sat, the details perduring
for decades after he'd read it, then scattered the ash in their garden
and how, decades after she'd left for the second-last last time, she'd forgotten
ever having typed it up in the desert, plotting her return.

LINES IN LVIV, FORMERLY LVOV, FORMERLY LEMBURG, NEAR LIMBO

The fine art of pretension, putting on airs
is exemplified by this, sitting in an outdoor café
on a chair tilting on cobblestones
watching the block-headed polity walk past,
hard starers every one of them,
cheerful and grim, indifferent to this sketching
which seems to slide easily into the sunlight
of a tree's blazing green head of hair
and the glowering sky, cool as a separation.
A clarinet, played well, breezes through the streets,
its notes as distinct and indistinct as turning inwards
once more, now the shouting in the square has died down
and the crowds are trudging back home, the earth relaxing
into its orbit once again. A dim sheen
rises now from the cobblestones as a pigeon inspects
each bump as thoroughly as a phrenologist.

It's like a giant family, being in a country
as monocultural, everyone a distant relation
except me. And that's fine.
I've examined myself in the mirror
and wouldn't dream of inflicting my relatedness
on anyone who didn't want it.
The telegraph wires are a nodal symphony
stretching across the street and sagging
into emptiness. Who wants to know about a poet
by his or her poetry? Wouldn't a blood test be easier,
or a DNA swab? Leave me out of it,
I'm just filling in time before I go.

2013

THE PROJECT

Let's shut it down.
Let's shut down the project.
There are protocols to be disregarded,
but don't shred the paperwork.
Let's allow it all to happen, slowly
but not as slow as an ice age.

But if it isn't our project
can we shut it down? Sure
we can, just like folding
the news up under an arm
then tossing it into the garbage.
But I'd like to return to the project.

I think we should shut it down.
I think it has run its course.
There are only so many efficiency dividends
and property keeps on rising. Bubbles
nibble the meniscus of my beer
which is further evidence of what

needs to be done: within the message
vacuity is necessary, and vacuity
is a dark attractor. Let's keep going
and keep this in mind. A tennis ball
ages like a middle-aged man
but middle-aged men are not tennis balls

even when they hit the net
trying to prove their relevance
like flies head-butting warm windows
or the dead sea of a white page filling with fly shit.

Ordinarily, that page would have been printed on
with schedules, memos, details of the project

but this no longer concerns us.
What matters is shutting down the project.
It no longer has a cost centre, but its costs
are incalculable. Shutting it down
is neither penny wise nor pound foolish:
it's entering the cave again, eyes wide open.

THE CAVE

opens into a blackened roof, veined
and drying, and out of it issuing
sighs or rattles. So small, and yet
it dominates the room. Wetting now and then
with swabs does nothing to slow down
the shallowing breath, the chill creeping
in from the limbs. Through it all, her eyes
stay open, seeing everything and nothing.

THE NARCOLEPT

The dinosaurs live on in chickens
and the dreams of an old woman
beached by an ocean of palsied sleep.

She's following their footprints back
to a time before sleep, roving
behind her eyelids, her soft palate

furling and unfurling like a flag.
For as long as I can remember, I lacked
confidence in consciousness. I'd watch

for ironing burning or pry open
sleeping eyes. Now it is the empty O
of agèd sleep drawing up alongside

death in that dream of ancient traffic,
those prehistoric footprints arrowing back
toward the start of the dream. Beyond extinction.

FILING CABINET

Kind of a coffin, it stands in my study, almost
as high and as wide. Its three drawers are shut,
flush with its front: wire and paper guts
in a wooden body. I don't know quite how to fill it:
God knows I've tried almost everything: genre, alphabet,
my different selves, the money spent. To keep it
satisfied, letters, faxes, poems, and bills
are never enough: it wants to annex the kingdom
of miscellaneous, which rules from paper towers
on top of it. It must be a family thing.
My mother was taxed in her later years
by paper taking over her house,
rearranging her mind in changing piles.
I'm much the same. Poetry is what escapes the files.

FIVE YEARS LATER

Seeing you today at the peace march, I could have slapped you
as you walked by and you wouldn't have seen it coming,
grey-green eyes absorbed in mournful hardness.
Charisma is a sponge
which sometimes needs wringing out.
Five years, I think, and now you're dyeing,
dressing still like twenty-somethings dress,
but thicker through the middle, calves like ninepins.
I thought I'd see a baby at your hip,
but you were alone, with another.
Compassion is less honest than intimacy.
At one with the crowd, I watched you swell
up George Street to the park
where you settled on the grass
and glittered in the heat. Then I came home.
There was no peace, or explanation:
such privacy, in public.
The sun went on trepanning the sky.

2003

THE ASH FIELD

1. The Phone Call from China

You can tell by its garden the rented house:
hardy perennials, the lawn resentfully shaved
and gutters backed up with gossip.
Nevertheless it's home, musty
in winter, a yeasty
ferment in summer.
It's hard not to remember it
as it became: emptied out,
a wardrobe's worth of shoes
left for litter. All the walls were lined with books,
the evenings Chinese whispers
until one of them became a squall.

2. Naked

If she could have slept, she might have dreamed of me
as I dreamed of her, or at least her absent shape.
I was in that house and there were rooms I'd never seen before
full of trappings and possessions I didn't know
belonged to her. The world came in to inspect it.
Someone gave me a veil – to wear or to escape in?
If I had been mere bones, I couldn't have been more naked.
It's because the world always already knows
and we're the ones who find out last of all.

3. Trees

The trees are full of tinnitus and light.
A fat fly walks lazily down the stem
of a vine to shade itself. The cortex
of the she-oak slowly wakes into a skink.
The morning air smells damp and burnt, skeined
with the wool of the smouldering log
still going from last night. Grey heat
glows at its edges, breathing smoke.
The she-oak is ancient and eyed with lost limbs,
the little lizards ascending and descending
like angels or truncated rivers striped with light.
The low-hanging clouds threaten a hostile takeover
of the smoke, but settle for my beard.
Is it true that a mirror decays?

4. Numb and Number

Quhilk is begun with inconstance,
And endis nocht but variance,
Scho haldis with continuance
            No serviture.
– William Dunbar, 'Inconstancy of Luve'

Which is worse: wasting years
in a labyrinth of grief, faithful
as an old boot, or brushing it off
like a cobwebbed leaf on a sleeve
or a mis-named fact?

Both will get you to where you're headed.

Take 'the phone call from China'.
Back then, I never got to see the number
but it wasn't who she said it was that deranged her:
not the suicide of a spurned lover in Singapore
or Bad Uncle, who'd shuffled off some years before,
but you, you piece of shit – I should explain:
'piece of shit' is a metaphysical term, denoting
a pigment of the imagination
which gets trekked in from the misremembered past
to stain the present, reminding with its stench
that there's always an outside to every intimation;
one synonym is 'carnal over-reach',
'numbness of the censors' is another –
and since we'll never speak again,
it's time to call you out, piece of shit,
as now at last I have your number:

you're the kind that has to keep on taking,
smart-arsed clerk, your family not enough,
numbing all around you without shame.
Now, you linger in my present.
Having taken what I once thought was my past, I'm glad
you leave me nothing.

I clean my shoe.

THE ANALYST

It's not the ziggurat
of DSMs and textbooks piled on the desk
nor the flag of surrender, waving feebly
from the adjacent box of tissues;
it's not the suggestion that any occupation
other than poet would be preferable,
financially and spiritually speaking,
nor the age difference, objectively speaking,
nor the speaking cure at which she believes she excels;
it's not the sharkskin sky
nor the gutter pattering softly as the snare
in Al Green's 'Take Me to the River';
but the way my analyst's dewlaps quiver
with all the inward pleasure
of revealing her entrancement by my ex
(apparently they haven't gotten to me yet).

NINE CRAB BARN

I made my way to Nine Crab Barn
and found there all the details of my brief:
curate the present, facilitate, on no account
create or show signs of belief.

All the people that I loved
were at a near remove, some near the bar,
others at the exits talking, making jokes,
some pleased to see me, some in fear

of something they refused to see
in me, or in themselves: the hair-trigger
which goes off on the freeway and makes a ute
carousel in elegant figures

of eight and greet a safety rail
like a love-tap or a peck on the cheek gone wrong.
I didn't drive but swam as briskly as the moon
in cloud at night, partly hidden in song-

light, laughing. Nine Crab Barn –
I'd heard the name before, a whispered spell
incanted over whiskey or set in circus fonts
on posters in the Star Hotel

and mentioned in biographies

of the Selfish Generation. Nine Crab Barn,
where it all once happened, where customers still sat
savouring the Great Man's yarn

of what went on, with whom, and when,
the mythology of proper names. I
would say *get fucked* to the lot of them, sycophants
and jerks and jumped-up literati

but then again, that's the problem
        I went there in the first place to address:
                the way mood shifts instantly from ecstasy to hate,
the way we fail our otherness.

Even though I'd never seen
        Nine Crab Barn before, I knew it well.
                It was capital of all the lost cost collectors
of the love-you hate-me soul.

Through the wave-crests, through the bottom
        of a schooner, through its sails, I'd
                dreamed it, through the foil-bright harbour baffling dusk
I'd dreamed it on the failing tide

of modern gentleness and hurt.
        It's where I came to learn the following home-grown
                truths: that every motorist is a satirist finding in traffic
every failing but her own;

that every day will have its dog;
        too many crooks (or is that cocks?) spoil
                the brothel. The homespun is an undecidable thing,
and means whatever you want to be real.

I arrived at Nine Crab Barn bang on midnight
        in doubting moonlight, its rooms ablaze with pleasure,
                music like a snake in flight from a jukebox yelling
into the night's black ear.

I found my room and dumped my bags
        and joined in unforgiving, blaring light
                all those others, all those I had loved and failed.
Now it is the place I write.

2014

FIRE

The only thing that travels faster than light
is its shadow: systems in eclipse
or the failure of an ancestor
hurtling out of the past to nobble a future.
Fire at a distance
is an index of love –
bright fire falling over buildings,
over heritage sandstone and embryonic gardens,
honing its shadows, the streetlight
rippling across the uneven lawn
or a truck's high beam lifting a driver's head
and punting it into darkness. Fire inside
meets fire from afar, a puddle
rises to soften the sun or a spider
springs into light, levering across its web,
and shadows onto its prey.
The fire inside you
radiates in all directions
and the shadow it casts from me
is where I have always been
but now will never go.

CURTAINS

Today there is a surfeit of light
and the curtains in the flat opposite
spread out of the window like an apron.

Two drunks, still going from last night,
dance slow dactylics on the street,
trying to hail a cab. Acorns of light

are planted everywhere
and invisible oaks rise up, spreading boughs
of heat. Traffic gnarls

and is combed out by the street.
Today is Sunday, a goat,
the day after Satyrday,

leaping from rock to rock
of the imagination, like surfing the net,
or surfing the light on a wave of heat.

Later, one curtain is blown back in
exposing a black guitar case
and its clasp, a cool gleam.

BEIJING DECTETS

reflection I

whatever words I have come back
as burred tokens relief worn smooth
or sound with a sense only partly for me
the city a set of controlled mirrors
shopfront windscreen commerce
heavenly haze miasma cigarette fug
or dry dust-fog a pedestrian tunnel under the freeway
leads to the metro a pony stands near the entrance
harnessed to the day selling mulberries
blackberries spiral-peeled pineapples

reflection II

voluntaries of sunlight dog the river
a vortex here a dimpling furrow there
what's the difference canal or paved river?
timber-knotted currents whorl and glitter
offering up the sky in mosaic flow
under the bridges a compost of midges
a fishing line's sagging hypotenuse
in contrapuntal flow rival yellow
blue and orange bicycles move midway
above the canal below the rumbling road

LII

In my fifty-third year towards heaven, my beard
shot through with white, like tissue-flecked washing,
I removed myself to the Northern Capital
to spend my days in study and contemplation
communing with nature on CCTV 2
far from the poisoned coteries and cliques
where judgements are capricious, bitter
and absolute as those of the ancient gods;
I prefer the problems of being alien,
provincial and unique; a foxed mirror.

question

some days the light finds me
like a grinch devoid of grace
the streets hemmed in haze a bare tree
asks a question bicycles and scooters
turning cars the heavy sooting trucks, long buses
give their answers the sun is a distant wen
seeping onto buildings easily discerned
in white and grey air thickens into
willow buds: heads of sparse hair
dreaded with green rising from tufted earth

mullock

my thinking is done in pacing dodging
wet islands of sputum
a quincunx of strawberries one corner of it squashed
over cracked pavers skirting mullock
which is the thinking of composition

barrages for the human rapids
who are at home here walking beside the calm
canal drooping willows a tranny ablaze
in a paved recess an aged couple
ballroom dancing in the gloom

blossoming

Spring is the deeper way than freeways
and smog under the hood
there are systems and redundancies
and for two weeks flowers opening
plane tree fuzz above our heads
and in our throats a prickling foil
such burgeoning requires deep soil
thick genetic rivers perfectly muddied
with you away this place is a delicious
prison such pleasure in discovering

facemask

a facemask becomes me so that only by my eyes
can I be known I become a facemask
shuffled out among cities streets lanes
and restaurants I will know them
as the canulating veins in my wrists knuckles
ciliae destroyed by endless smog know numbers
for the verities and vices inconstant moonlight
consumption and decay by rectifying
the incongruity of names lies the future
swipe down to search swipe left to like

tomb sweeping (qingming) I

Gēge runs the show in Tiger Hollow
    the hills behind the hamlet
where my father-in-law grew up
    his house   a cottage of one or two rooms
we are the ring-ins   me and the little boy
    on a matrilineal line   following Gēge's lead
we'll end up at the plots   the living have reserved
    later we'll eat cousin Lĭ Liúfú's organic food
bamboozled in equal measure   by the table-talk
    in sūsònghuà   and by the báijiŭ

tomb sweeping (qingming) II

tumulus by tumulus   we let off bungers
    and poured out wine   for the Lĭ family dead
burned hell banknotes for those who starved to death
    or died of old age   the grass soughs
but nothing stirs in the undergrowth
the freeway only metres away
as we kowtow to the past   the dead know more
    than we do   like where we'll be
in a century   and how the light here
    sharpens everything on time's lathe

smokescreen

spring's method is surprise:
a green glimmer mingling
smokeflowers with bloodblossoms,

dirty cool air with a hot sun.
In a couple of weeks it's over:
all the trees luxuriate in green

and the wind harvests voices
from the leaves. All this is smoke-
screen for the work it's done in you

this little nub of ours   this autumn bloom

WARATAH

Then the Giant-killer handed me a herb he had plucked from the ground, and showed me what it was like. It had a black root and a milk-white flower. The gods call it Moly, and it is an awkward plant to dig up, at any rate for a mere man. But the gods, after all, can do anything.

– Book X: Circe, *The Odyssey*, trans. E.V. Rieu

1.

I'm clearing a space in Waratah.
Here, in Waratah, I'm making a clearing,
marking out space among bluetongues, grevilleas,
a conurbation of ants' nests. I'm making a space
the size of a mid-range imagination,
a modest keep, a distillation of hope.
I'm chucking out, I'm ringing in, and I'm wiping clean
here in Waratah, leaving a burly wake. I'm stacking
and hanging, playing and putting away: Dada to one side,
Villa-Lobos the other, the Velvets and Cesar Vallejo,
Li Bai, *Satura*, Pantagruel feasting in Paris. Somewhere
among these, to one side, maybe just over the way
I'm clearing more spaces in Waratah. Here.

2.

There's a brawl of clouds over Kooragang.
White on grey, duck egg on magnetite, piled up high on each other,
stacking up like a freeway disaster. All day, inland heat
has been steepling, stifling the river. Up through the palms
a quiver of Chisel, magpie bubble-song, backyard breezes
outing their bounds, shouldering their way through vines,
making their way to this space I'm clearing in Waratah.
I'm growing a thousand lanterns curled in bright green shade,
chandeliers of tucked seahorse, an oast of spice
as hot as the early summer heat. I'm clearing a space for them too.

3.
George Thomas Ferris, I'm back here in Waratah.
John Blake Quealy, I'm here in my clearing.
Respectful as a body of undertakers
aloof from a family's grief, the currawongs
confer on the nature strip opposite, stepping daintily on scaly feet
or supine, receiving the beak of a mate, rampant with grey fluffy breast.
Wintergrass, buffalo, paspalum, couch niggle over the lawn,
carpet my clearing with their bladed relations.
Dorothy Downs Pawsey, I'm back here in Newcastle.
Eliza Augusta Prentice, I'm just down the road.

4.
I'm building a structure of time and air,
mortared by sound. I'm piecing it together,
here in the shadow of the Moly-Cop mastaba,
flanged by the two-carriage whistle of Maitland trains.
In the smoke-quiet streets of Waratah, you can see people
smoking moly in rollies, dealing moly in parks;
in The Town Hall, the Royal, in Waratah Park,
the hushed business of moly. Property prices
go hand in hand with molyfication. That's why the Moly-Cops
are just down the road, regulating, confiscating, keeping it all
in hand. But I'm with Gryllus on that one, I never touch the stuff.
I prefer to stay as I am, snuffling around.

5.

Across from ours, a weatherboard house
and a Woolworths shopping trolley parked on the nature strip,
Newcastle trees, angophora, turpentine, palings the colour of old bone.
A brown bluetongue suns itself. Carers of the old and dying
come and go in shifts. The steelworks shriek intermittently,
minting and banging. Threading the clangour of industry,

a long train of portbound extinction.
Mynahs attack the bluetongue; a baby currawong
shivers on the Hills Hoist. Hail and tar, fledgling leaves,
the scratch of lungsmoke wood-burning.

6.
I'm pitching a tent in the blue field of death.
The spring maggies swoop, spiteful
as early Mick Jagger lyrics, and just as lively.
The frangipanis peep out little green horns,
leaf-hooks and spiderwebs furtive with death.
A powerful owl monsters the baby currawong,
the mynahs shit on the roof. Lorikeets
and wattlebirds pilfer the bright red bottlebrush flower,
tweeting their restaurant reviews. Silence
is everywhere else but here, in Waratah.

7.
I'm adding my bit to the Waratah Symphony.
I'm tempering my piano, running my fingers over its keys,
good teeth and bad teeth, major and minor.
I'm tuning the strings, composing a private cantata,
savouring note after note in a climacteric
of joy. I'm painting the space I'm clearing
with low humid sounds and high nips of light.
Now, we're inkling the air with song, we're singing
here, in Waratah, a piece for love and piano
in the key of near. We're clearing a space for song.

京禧

I perform a Vulcan mind-meld on my son
who's only two weeks old, but quite receptive.
As I touch his forehead, his eyelids close
like two shelled almonds.
I see alabaster mountains
topped with porphyry, a chorus
of light and fuzzy dark,
teething curves, milky ecstasies...
I can't tell what Jingxi sees in me: he shifts
a little uncomfortably, his brow
ridges, then he screams.

INFORMATION THEORY 2

I have this little piece of information.
It weighs about eight kilograms.
Its fingers, toes are just like mine
but its consciousness of each of them isn't.

I call it 'information'. It calls me 'oo-wa'
sometimes, at other times just 'waa'.
It has a low tolerance for redundancy
and a preference for entropy.

Its skin is a pinguid resin
of amino acids, capillaries and down.
It forages in my delight
and smells like an unwashed mouse.

THE TRANSPORTATIONS OF GEORGE BRUCE

We were naked.
We watched, from the thick part of the woods,
the police take the others away. It was raining,
the depth of winter, the sky black as loss,
the trees of our camp aglow with the fire
which had warmed us. There had been five of us
untimely mortals plus our Judas, who was spared,
leaving Meredith, Farr and me. The other two hanged.

At the midnight hour I'd heard the snapping of twigs,
the stamp of boots, and woke my two companions.
We were wanted for thieving Government stock,
for each of us had escaped the hand of the tyrant
for the employ of a settler, for whom we thieved by night
from all the settlements. Our Judas had made a pact
with the police, jumping the fire with the two who hanged
while we went the other way into darkness.

I knew my way to the ends of the colony.
I had worked for Doctor Caley, while yet a boy
collecting insects: trap-door spiders and caterpillars
as thick as an index finger, covered with crimson hairs
that break off into your skin when touched, as sin does;
summer beetles which shine as though enchased with gold;
twigs which move without wind and resolve into limbs
and bodies, heads and feelers atwitch with knowledge of God.

I set down by a large tree with the two untimely creatures
and remained there until morning. My joints then set
with cold, so that I could not rise without help.
We threaded the thick wood south, following a reedy stream
aslant with ribbons of eels and fulsome with crickets and frogs

towards Prospect where there lived a man I thought I could trust
with my life. I had no fear even though we were deathly cold
with shrivelled privates, our feet torn as if desiring thorns.

In a day and a night we made it to Luker's
but as soon as I entered his house I saw by his wry countenance
that he had a Judas heart and the Devil had locked his jaw.
But the Grand Arch Angel with flaming sword in hand
was guarding my poor sinful soul, and so his wife shifted him
off to Towngabby to see George Pell for clothing for us three.
She gave us a large cake of flour and a good piece of pork
as we lamented our horrid state, ruinous as wolves.

We set out once more for the house of Joshua Peck
through a dale of yellowed stumps like filed down teeth.
I made thanks to Merciful God who had brought us from the gulf of Hell
and delivered us from the tyrant, and snakes and wild beasts
that would devour a man. My companions tired of my preaching.
Soon we were at the house of Peck, who received us most efficaciously.
Mr Peck brought us some rags to cover our nakedness
and Mrs Peck told us that Luker had gone to inform on us.

We took our leave of these bright souls, and as Sister Peck had suggested,
we climbed the hill behind them, and from there saw Luker
and thirty untimely creatures dancing around the house of loving Peck
like the Serpent around the Garden of Job
when God permitted Job's temptation.
Then I arose and Farr asked where I was going.
I said I would go wherever the blessed Lord Jesus Christ pleased,
for as he brought the Children of Israel through the Wilderness

so the Redeemer would bring us through these sinuous and prickly woods.
We took the road to the Hawkesbury and travelled the night in silence.
We arrived at ten o'clock. Among the settlers Farr discovered one he knew
who said we could not stay, for the police and soldiers were expected.

I was given a cake and a piece of pork to carry,
but had only gone so far before my companions slipped away.
I was by myself. I went to the side of a large lagoon
where I lay down and grief overcame me. I thought my soul was melting.

I sought a sign from the Heavenly King, which would not be my first, nor last
Eight years before when I lived with the Superintendent of Towngabby
I was watching his house at midnight when I saw my own person
stand before me, clear as clear, and say *So wonderful*
shall all men be when they hear of the miracles
God shall work with you in this life. At these words
I closed my eyes. When I opened them again, it was gone.
Cold sweat coursed through my hair and down my face in torrents.

This was my poor immortal soul leapt out of her chamber.
But now her seat was usurped by one of Satan's imps
so that on her return she had no place to rest, only bare walls
to cling to like a bat on a white sheet at night.
But a powerful angel that overlooks poor weak souls like mine
was passing and heard her pitiful cries, rebuked the evil spirit
and gave my soul her seat. This was the first of the signs
that proved a species of transportation. Nor am I free of these signs.

Even now in Greenwich as I relate this part of my life
three of the Beelzebub gang jump up in my room, demanding I go
with them to their master. All three look like an old and tame baboon
I once saw playing with a child. When the child smacked it
on the head, the baboon would twinkle his eyes
and focus up his mouth as if sucking plums. Such are the faces
of these demons, filled with infernal lies by the Serpent,
which they soon vomit up, leaving me in peace.

Suddenly a body of geese, about six or seven thousand
appeared in the sky and descended so low I beheld them
perfectly white as snow. The lagoon was about three miles around

and these beautiful creatures covered one, making their circuit thrice
as if Jehovah had made a string fast to each and was playing with them
out of the window of Heaven. A whispering voice said
Do not despair, behold the road thou art to take this day.

In astonishment I saw the birds cluster in a shady place
then straight as a line they followed each other into the scarlet darkness.
I set out through the woods in the same direction as nigh as I could
and soon met a man who asked my business. I said I was gone
to banish myself from all society. Tears rolled down his cheeks.
I remained with him three weeks, during which time we learned
of the hanging of Farr and Meredith. Then I returned to my desert days
where it was ordained that I should wander in my transported state.

At last I met the man who preserved my life, good Gilberthorpe.
He took me to a large hollow tree at the back of his farm
where I remained some time. Each night I burned the trees off his land
until I cut my foot most dreadfully planting wheat in moonlight.
For fourteen days I remained where my friend had placed me
until my bandage fell off and my wound had closed
but I had lost the use of my right side. Good Gilberthorpe
brought his wife to see me, fearing that I would die.

I told them not to despair, that I would not die yet
by grace of the signs that God had shown me.
I told them of meeting my soul that time in Towngabby
and another sign shown me at dead of night
when the skies parted asunder and the light of heaven
was just like the light from a broken lamp
through the cracks of a door, shining no further
than where I lay. A voice said the Lord had heard my prayers,

that my life shall be recorded through all nations
and that those who hate me shall fear me. Then the heavens closed.
A third sign was in a dream where I fell down a steep hill

and came with great violence against an iron stanchion
which shook me so much I said that this was no dream.
There was a man by the side of these rails and I asked
what place this was. Under the rails there appeared to be a furnace
at full heat. *This is Hell*, he said, but yet no person was in it.

A fourth was a dream where I went to a house
with windows in the top of it, one of which was open,
and three Grand Angels were in the house, and three Goddesses.
I advanced to a glass case full of otherworldly jewels
and while I stood gazing, the Goddesses came to me,
and pointing to a gold crown covered with diamonds
the centre one said that this crown was for me.
I proceeded to a large table spread with something white

and the Goddess told me it was the canopy of heaven
and I must eat my belly full. And as I was eating
a beautiful man passed by the table, and the Goddess said
it was the Grand Arch Angel that brought the canopy
for me to eat. I watched him ascend through the window
at the top of the house and the Angels and Goddesses followed.
The next day Gilberthorpe came and laid me on the bole
of an old dead tree where I would be exposed to the sun

for the best part of the day, my lame side upmost.
Each night he came to remove me, repeating the same
until at the end of six weeks I recovered the use of my side
and began to walk again. For five months I remained with Gilberthorpe,
working at night and sleeping in daytime beside a beautiful stream
until the new Governor arrived, whose name was Philip Gidley King.
My friend Gilberthorpe went to him and told him of all my suffering
and how for five months he knew me to be hard at work.

The Governor straight away granted my pardon
and received me as if I had been one of his own children.
He was pleased to order me to New Zealand,
where I remained for seven months.
I lived there among the inhabitants, and consented
to be marked in the face when I received my wife.
She and my child have now been dead for years
and I have since grown used to the solitude of grief.

CHYORT

Eye-deep in pollen I strode across the plain, cubed
by star pickets and their slack cross-hatchings,
sun-blind and sweating, the chunked city smoked
out of green fog, dodged traps and skirted trees brushing

a sky-powdered moon, sank ankle-deep in a dam's
dark border and witnessed the splashed rising of birds
and a frightened trotting of sheep, the spume
of silent aircraft knotted in thin white cords above,

heard the hiss of road trains braking, their savage
road-thundering, earth freshly ripped and steaming,
the sluggard river clay-bright and oozing
into cracked banks, stepped through a rust harvest

of doorless cars and a ripple of tattered barns,
through fields of scattered cardboard, bound
newspapers, slashed and slithery vinyl
chairs and a chipped glossy dog, tailless

and began to climb, fingernails dark rotting
crescents, up flesh-coloured sides thickly
reeking moist garbage, rasped knees
on sandstone polyhedrons and lodged boots squarely

under peeling roots and then rucked clear and strove
towards the mantle of sky scummed with cloud, dragged
back with each step in a skitter of fresh, pale rocks
and crabbed free, edging closer, ever as far.

FROM A TRAIN IN CONNECTICUT

Petrillo's Used Auto Parts just outside New Haven
contains about a thousand newish cars
all wrecked, rusting, with tyreless wheels
and cataracted windscreens.
There's not a soul in sight, just the river
flowing slowly in mild lobes
swapping one bank for another.
In his office sits Joe Petrillo, worried about his weight
and listening to the radio, sweating
on the Mets getting back their stars
in time for the playoffs.

Centuries ago near what became New Haven
the Quinnipiac and the Pequot fought a series of battles
or skirmishes, really, the Quinnipiac coming off second best,
eventually selling their land to some Europeans
in exchange for a peace of sorts.
Nearby, firs serry up a hill, just as near Munich,
where not as long ago there was a similar appeasement.
It's hard to imagine. It seems so peaceful here,
although the creeping greenery is an intimation
of violence, full of life and humid intent.

Last night Joe dreamt he'd killed his oldest friend,
years ago, and had been getting away with it all this time.
Awake, he remembers that he has not seen him
for several years now, not since the friend moved
to Mystic, Connecticut. Or was that a mistake?
Perhaps there's blood on his hands after all.
He can't be sure, now, in the wide hours
of early morning, unbalanced accounts
before him in a yet to be ordered pile.

This is the problem, not his business or his weight
but that he never seems to coincide
with himself. Whenever he finds himself,
it's always provisional, like a ford
in a rising river. Most of all he is afraid.
The shuttered sun serrates the room.

2013

THE POTATO

One or the other of us will have to go,
my father said, eyeing the last potato.
The last of its kind, for the moment, it sat on a plate,
the last of its kind, broken up from a deceased estate
scattered through antique shops and distant relatives
and patterned with its own objective correlative:
Koong Se walks behind the garden wall
worried about her imminent betrothal
to some Duke; meanwhile, her lover Chang
schemes to lure her into his Ford Mustang
or at least his dynasty's version of it: a souped-up Sampan
with modified oars and a comfy bridal suite. His flight plan
is simple enough: to an island where he and Koong Se will co-habit
and he will become famous for his writings. They will breed like rabbits.
What does Koong Se have to say about all this? She dreams
about Chang almost every night, of floating away downstream
and even though, the story goes, they elope,
she'd never leave her father or push the envelope
of filial piety, even if she had ever existed
instead of being part of some ham-fisted
chinoiserie from the land of intrepid explorers
and the agents of the potato's diasporas.
If it wasn't for the outbreak of potato blight
Ireland wouldn't have halved itself overnight
and my father's great-great-grandfather
wouldn't have come here with a brother
and two sisters who would scatter
to Mudgee, Berry, Parramatta,
Bathurst and beyond. There wouldn't have been me
playing with Mister Potato Head, somewhat pudgy
at three or four, plugging in a nose or an ear –
O where are the Mister Potato Heads of yesteryear?

Perhaps that's why it is the most human of vegetables:
we gouge its eyes out, stick it in the oven, then on a table
as I did later, serving my father his beloved potato.
Of course, he was the first to go.

2014

HOSPITAL

My deathbed has not yet been made
but has been manufactured
in a plant in Guangdong province

primarily by a man called Qing
who plays left halfback in the fourth grade
and is expert on the pressing machine.

We have common ancestors, Qing and I,
a man called Gan who lived in central Asia
and died in the year of the dog,

in the year of long rains and pestilence,
lying on a bed of camel-skin,
his fever abated somewhat by water

given him by my ancestor, Gan's daughter
who later married into the tribe of the red bear
then disappeared into the west

while Qing's ancestor, Gan's son
slaughtered a goat
and offered its blood to the wind god

and left its flesh to the elements,
having seen the good
that comes from tending to the dying.

HOMECOMING

Sun-damaged, sporty, wearing tracky-daks,
passengers can't be told from cabin crew
apart from their uniforms, their Australian chilliness;
          hedonists mostly,

serious adepts of *physis*, puritanical,
wary of alien cuisines, monolingual –
all of them start relaxing as cabin crew cross-check,
          landing gear lowers,

ailerons bristle, engines sough and earth climbs.
Longitude-trekkers, these new internationalists
humbled by nothing, not even their ignorance,
          chattering blithely,

wonder aloud how home has changed in their absence.
It hasn't, but they have. The world has reduced them to
miniature giants approaching a sparsely rich country,
          mulletocratic,

athlete-revering, distrustful of politics, obedient.
It's all about making money now, caring for investments as
if they were souls, or as if there was no such thing as a soul,
          or like, whatever.

Closer inspection, though, reveals great variety:
Shanghai-Chinese returning to investment properties;
Heibei tycoons, cashed up and itching to
          visit the casino;

taffy-haired surfers who get on at Cairns and stink of
wine-garlic night-before-breath; Euro-tanned

backpackers, double-chinned – even the fittest are
Maillol-limbed beauties;

experts in security returning from Guangzhou to
Punchbowl; aromatherapists fresh from new franchises;
teachers of English and commerce students back for
one more semester.

Where are the famous, the rich and powerful?
Prize-winning architects returning from Chengdu with the
Astrodome contract? Investment bankers from Stanmore?
Fact-finding pollies?

Business or first class, economy, it doesn't matter:
pig-tailed professionals or t-shirted, unkempt and
scolding their children, they all speak the same
vulgar-demotic.

Even the hosties are customers somewhere or other.
Difference is not really monetary – it's an asset. As
wheels kiss the tarmac, dawn strips them bare: so
ugly they're beautiful.

2010

WIRE

Why're we
yeah nah
weird how we're all wireless now
worried hedonists
yeah nah
meaning: yes I'm worried, no I'm not a hedonist, or
yes I am a hedonist, and because of that I'm worried, or
yes I am a hedonist, and consequently I'm not worried, or
yes I hear you and it's fucked
yeah nah
word has it wireless is better than being wired
only some of us are wired
and we celebrate that with razors
yeah nah
meaning: yes it's true that we detain them
but it's not me who done it, or
yeah, the razors are sharp
nah, it's not a celebration, innit? Or
yeah they must be baddies
nah, only kidding, or
yeah, it's true
nah, my wireless isn't working here
too much inference
yeah nah
means, it's true, but I can't see it
means it isn't real
Innit?
yeah nah

EXTINCTION

The two last speakers of the dying language
no longer talk to each other.

OIL: AN ELEGY

I.

It disappeared at the height of summer:
the highways were almost deserted
and the last sky-writing feathered into nothing.
Constipated clouds spat tiny drops
on smoking hills
and the hot winds ran on
across the deserts and bubbling roads,
baffling the cities and drubbing their glass scapes.

Hybrid cars misted the morning
and, smudge by smudge, smog disappeared.
Our lives shunted on. Hydrogen was farmed
from the sea, the wind yoked, sunlight harvested
and the boiling bowels of the earth went powering on;
but we had our last day as ourselves.

Now it is scattered through a billion skies;
the mantle of our dismantling;
but suburbia, which oil invented,
failed to mourn its passing, so busy
was the population waging war
on space and time. Then their words,
which had become so dense with oil and speed
discovered once more the air between them.

And in those days when the last rigs bloomed,
nostalgia ruled and all the motorists agreed
the day of its death was a major bummer.

2.

We went stupid on it: never where we wanted
to be, we used it up on fast-tracks to nowhere.
In the cities it gave us our daily bread.
It made possible the meeting of cornichons
with Incan woollens and Willy Wonka Bars.
It was the opposite of poetry:
oil made everything happen.
Now it lives on in the thermosphere
and flows through the pores of withered leaves
and lingers around the words of the living
like seas around bleached coral reefs;
poetry survived the incremental tide,
became a setting forth, thought's improvised canoe.

3.

Sky, receive our immolation –
the liquid states of the fossil nation;
receive into your greenhouse layers
the vanity of these, our prayers.

GLAMOUR

Sunset pinks the sportsman's bar
and dirty sweat glistens
like gold dust on their arms

as the drinkers listen
to the knowledgable drawl
of Smacker who, perched in a lipid sprawl

upon his stool, grades their conversation
with his steady tone, the master
of the stubble-scratch-and-frown,

a gesture he admired in Uncle Clem
and copied with apish diligence.
And by the others too – Smacker is their arbiter of elegance:

Dicko, for example, hawks his phlegm
and spits the way he's studied Smacker do it;
the way that Dicko rolls his sleeves

is copied by Chopper,
with the innovation of socks
at complementary half-mast,

now *de rigueur* for the lot.
How rich they seem in the gilding light:
the glittering, interlocking rings

left on the table by their drinks;
the lapidary condensation of their beers;
but richer still, the innocent ballet

of lumbering towards the bar,
a complicated dance whose artless steps
they've studied hard to master all these years.

THE MAN WHO LOVES POLICEMEN

You've seen him at the footy or the Easter Show,
wherever there's a crowd and its controls: neither
like you nor himself, arms crossed, having a matey chat

with a couple of cops as if they were his brothers-in-law
at a barbecue, and not the law pumped up in leather
jackets, sunglasses, limp batons at the hip.

He loves these conversations: shooting from the lip
about the common Aussie yobbo, his habitat
and how to tame him. He talks with unselfconscious grace

as if bestowing membership to the human race
on his protectors, but the put-down passes: nothing rankles,
not even faded leg iron scars around their ankles.

MOUNTAIN STREAM, ALTIPLANO

The earth channels the sky
in a kind of sweaty trance:
inching furrows, shallow
finger-diggings of rain and dew

fork in jagged tines across the plateau –
and then the river wrinkles
into a blue scour so rapid
and flat it seems to be flowing uphill.

What's weirder is mountains shouldering
into the massively empty valley
and across them, dark lightning of dry streambeds
striking upwards to the peaks.

THE LAKE

Words possess us
        with forgetfulness and love
makes us remember
        how to live: waking up
from dreams relieved
        the day does not flow
like the oneiric river

backwards up a hill,
        in one ear, out
another's, garbling
        onto the mirror
of the black lake
where every image

is a bullet from the future
        never seeming to break
the surface, a limited
indefinite remembering
the nothing beneath it,
        the black loveless nothing.

        That is the nightmare:
to dream of things
exactly as they are.

There was this lake. As clean as an eye but below its surface were sparse, slimy weeds. It was cold, much colder than the air and still as a pane of unbroken glass. It was the kind of place you went to to forget, only it was too shallow to let the past entirely disappear. Rowing out to the middle you found bits of yourself floating past, sinking slowly to the bottom or rising to the surface. Clouds were moving across the sky very quickly and their reflections were so big they almost capsized you. Still, you were happy enough: the entire world had become nothing more than the membrane upon which you drifted for what seemed like forever.

UNCOLLECTED

LETTER TO A DEAD PARENT

Whenever I look at your grandson,
I see dad's face, but you're the one
or several parts of one, who animates his rage
and cheek, just as how the other day
at two-and-a-quarter, he put a soccer ball
into a bucket and called it 'ice cream', licking it.
It's as if you're still alive, but blind to survival,
counting 'one, two, five, eighteen, twenty four'
with the precision of a train timetable,
opened at random. How you would have loved
to see him, even in your last unravelling,
the way he pushes away my hand
if I try to turn the page too soon, or how
he will stare blankly ahead, deaf to anything
I say before slyly looking sideways at me,
then laughing. This week I've drawn
fifty seven big fish and three hundred
and forty two little fish and thirty eight
spouting whales. It's hard to believe
that part of me could go on being, let alone
this tenacious chain that links to you, here,
where a breeze bends the corridor
around its cold and touches your hair.
A lot has happened since you've gone:
this pandemic; it's strange how there
are no individuals, just a society where
you can hide but can't run.
Your grandson brings me a horse's head
in the palm of his hand, separated from its body

by an accident, and overcome by penitence,
says 'sorry daddy' over and over, lying face down
on the ground. I didn't teach him this,
so where did he learn it? I'm sorry that you never got to see
his frown, breathing over a shark or Boss Boonga
in the Big House at the end of the road.
But when he points at agave plants
along the side path, tells me 'dinosaur'
I dine on sores, or dining saws remind me
of the older truths, the hardening of bone
or its mirror, sagging skin, a voice that's broken
into words, or words flowering into the wave
of a hand, 'goodbye outside, goodbye diningsaur'.

NOTES TO POEMS

'Ode to Michael Dransfield': Michael Dransfield, Australian poet (1948-1973).

'Glenrowan': the Glenrowan Hotel was the scene of the fateful siege between the Kelly gang and Victorian police in 1880. Gang members Dan Kelly, Steve Hart and Joe Byrne died in the siege, with Hart and Kelly burnt beyond recognition. Byrne, who died from a gunshot wound to the groin, was partially burnt, but not so bad as to be unable to be posed for photographs. Ned Kelly was injured during the siege, captured and later executed.

'Lagoon': The Lagoon, postcode 2795 is a small town on the western slopes of NSW. Typical of the area, it was populated by Irish convicts, among them my great-great-great-grandfathers Owen Guggrty (1818-1892), transported for highway robbery in West Meath and William Costello (1808-1855) transported for possession of a stolen lamb in Galway.

'Blackheath': Blackheath, a town in the Blue Mountains west of Sydney.

'Australian Beach Pattern': the title is of a famous painting by Charles Meere (1890-1961) from 1940, so hideous it's somewhat appealing.

'Young Montaigne Goes Riding': imagery largely taken from the E. V. Rieu translation of Montaigne's essays.

'Death by Water 1': 'Had [Mackellar] reached England he could well have profoundly altered Macarthur's career, and through this the course of Australia's history.' M. Austin, *Dictionary of Australian Biography*, Volume

2 (Melbourne UP, 1967); '*helped drag two bodies out of the Cudgegong River …*' from 'Joe Wilson's Courtship' by Henry Lawson (1867-1922), Australian poet and short story writer; Harry Albury was Lawson's maternal grandfather. At the time of writing I was blithely unaware of the wacky coincidence that Stephen Tuckerman, a Nantucketer, whose maternal grandfather was also lost at sea, was related to some of T.S. Eliot's ancestors and several of Ezra Pound's.

'Wet Season': Port Hedland, WA.

'Reading Laurie Duggan in the Shanghai New Zhen Jiang Restaurant': '*It's death, my aunt says, and he's/reading your poems.*' From Laurie Duggan's poem 'What I Came Onto' from *Adventures in Paradise* (Little Esther, 1991).

'Anatomy of Voice': in part an elegy to Bill Maidment (1924-2005), an influential teacher at the University of Sydney. The poem is a livre composé, divided into four partitions after Robert Burton's *Anatomy of Melancholy*.

'Coastline': 'taghairm' is a method of divination involving sewing a person into the hide of a freshly-killed ox which was then placed beside a waterfall or other desolate place, to enable the person to foresee the outcome of an impending battle; the oracle of the hide.

'The Narcolept': my mother, Elizabeth Anne Musgrave, née Quealy (1933-2016) suffered from narcolepsy and cataplexy for most of her adult life.

'Beijing Dectets': *qingming* (清明), also known in English as Tomb Sweeping Day, is a traditional Chinese festival which falls on the first day of the fifth solar term of the traditional Chinese calendar. This makes it the 15th day after the Spring Equinox, either the 4th or 5th of April in any given year. During *qingming*, Chinese families visit the tombs of their ancestors to clean the gravesites, pray to their ancestors, and make ritual offerings, which typically include food and wine, the burning of joss sticks and hell banknotes (these are joss paper notes solely intended as burnt offerings to the deceased as a superstitious solution to resolve ancestors' financial problems; some are actually printed in China with the words 'Hell Banknotes' in English on them), and the lighting of firecrackers.

gēge (哥哥), older brother.

báijiŭ (白酒), Chinese white wine.

sūsònghuà (宿松话) is the dialect spoken in Susong county, Anhui province.

'Waratah': suburb of Newcastle, NSW. 'Chisel' refers to Cold Chisel, Australian rock band. George Thomas Ferris (1838-1903), the paternal grandfather of my paternal grandmother, resident in Waratah in 1866 at the time of his marriage. John Blake Quealy (1902-1978), great uncle who lived in Waratah in the 1930s. Dorothy Pawsey, née Downs (1791-1832), my 4th great-grandmother arrived in NSW in 1827 and died in Newcastle in 1832. Her daughter Eliza Augusta Prentice, née Pawsey (1822-1900), George Ferris's mother-in-law and my 3rd great-grandmother lived in and around Maitland all her adult life.

Moly-Cop: from its factory in Waratah, Moly-Cop manufactures the Comsteel product range of rail consumables.

Gryllus: the companion of Odysseus who refused to be returned to human form from that of a pig. See Plutarch's 'Beasts are Rational' (Περὶ τοῦ τὰ ἄλογα λόγῳ χρῆσθαι — Bruta animalia ratione uti) from his *Moralia*.

京禧: 京 is the 'jīng' in Běijīng, meaning 'capital'. 禧 or 'xǐ' means auspiciousness, happiness or jubilation. 京禧 is a homophone of 惊喜, which means 'pleasantly surprised'.

'The Transportations of George Bruce' is adapted from two transcripts of the manuscript *Life of a Greenwich Pensioner 1776-1817*, one by Benedict Taylor and the other compiled by Thomas Whitley pre-1898. Grace Karskens refers to the Benedict Taylor transcript numerous times in *The Colony*, noting that 'Convicts were reported as working without clothes in the heat' (Allen & Unwin 2009); however, Bruce's story suggests that it was in winter that the raid took place on his gang. Although it may be that convicts worked without clothes at times in imitation of the Eora, Bruce's manuscript makes no mention at all of the indigenous inhabitants of the colony.

'Chyort': (чёрт) is the Russian word for 'devil'.

'Extinction': in 2011 this situation was reported with regard to the two last speakers of the language Ayapaneco in Mexico.

'The Potato': my father's great-great-grandfather Thomas Bernard L'Estrange (1819-1856): see 'Death by Water 1'.

'Oil: An Elegy' is written after Auden's 'In Memory of W.B. Yeats'.

ACKNOWLEDGEMENTS

I would like to express my deep appreciation to Alex Wylie for his editing of this book and Todd Swift and the Eyewear team for their generosity in publishing it. I'd also like to thank Peter Kirkpatrick, Ken Bolton and John Watson for their help in making the selections for this volume.

CPSIA information can be obtained
at www.ICGtesting.com
Printed in the USA
FSHW011333100921
84631FS

9 781913 606121